The Adopter's Handbook on Education

GETTING THE BEST FOR YOUR CHILD

Eileen Fursland

coramBAAF
ADOPTION & FOSTERING ACADEMY

Published by
CoramBAAF Adoption and Fostering Academy
41 Brunswick Square
London WC1N 1AZ
www.corambaaf.org.uk

Coram Academy Limited, registered as a company limited by guarantee
in England and Wales number 9697712, part of the Coram group,
charity number 312278

British Library Cataloguing in Publication Data
A catalogue record for this book is available from the British Library

ISBN 978 1 910039 70 0

Project management by Miranda Davies, CoramBAAF
Designed by Helen Joubert Design
Printed in Great Britain by The Lavenham Press

Trade distribution by Turnaround Publisher Services, Unit 3, Olympia
Trading Estate, Coburg Road, London N22 6TZ

Contents

Acknowledgements

First, I would like to offer my thanks and gratitude to Shaila Shah and CoramBAAF for commissioning me to write this book and to Miranda Davies for guiding through each stage of its journey to publication. Thanks also to Sonia Jackson for reading and making helpful comments on the draft.

Miranda has simultaneously been editing a companion book on education for children in care, by Sarah Alix and Alan Fisher, which will be published later this year. I have been able to adapt some of their material about the education system for use in the Appendix to this book, and I am grateful to them for that.

There are many talented individuals and committed organisations working hard to advance our knowledge and increase awareness of what helps adopted children in school and bring about change, either in their schools or more widely. I would like to think that this book recognises their valuable work and brings it together in a way that will be useful to adoptive parents. I have quoted a number of them throughout the book. PAC-UK and Adoption UK, for example, which work tirelessly to improve adopted children's lives, have been at the forefront and have kindly given permission for me to include some of their information here for parents.

This book has been informed by the research, campaigning and professional expertise of adoption and other support organisations, academic institutions, educationalists and experts and the insights and experiences of adoptive parents and adopted young people – all of whom play a vital role in increasing our understanding of what adopted children need in school. Sadly no longer with us is the late Gareth Marr, who campaigned long and hard for local authority virtual schools to support the education of adopted children as well as those in care, which has now become a reality.

Many people have shared their knowledge, their stories and their experiences with me, or have kindly given me permission to quote their work. I'd like to give credit to everyone who has informed the thinking behind the book, but they are too numerous to mention here so I'll limit myself to extending my thanks in particular to: Michael Bettencourt, Julia Brown, Sally Donovan, Jennifer Ginger, Stuart Guest, Emily Hamblin, Helen Hoban, Claire Hiorns and the Cambridgeshire Virtual School, Nicola Marshall, Cherry Newby and Jennifer Nock; and those adoptive parents who gave their time to speak to me, to comment on the draft and contribute their own thoughts (thank you, Karen Wilkins) and/or who kindly allowed me to include extracts from their blogs and personal accounts. The voices of adopted young people come from, among others: Coram Adoptables, AT-ID and a remarkable group of young people who shared their personal experiences at Adoption UK's annual conference (on education) in 2017.

The driving force behind the book is all of you adoptive parents out there. You, more than anyone, know how important it is to find ways to support children in school and to work with teachers and others to help make it a nurturing environment in which each child can thrive.

About the author

Eileen Fursland is a freelance writer specialising in issues affecting children and young people. She has written extensively for BAAF, and now CoramBAAF, on a number of publications since 2002, as well as for a range of magazines and national newspapers and other organisations.

Eileen's publications for BAAF include the training course *Preparing to Adopt* (she wrote the first edition in 2002 with a working party from BAAF which devised the course, and the fourth edition, 2014, with Nicky Probert and Elaine Dibben); her books *Facing up to Facebook* (second edition 2013); *Social Networking and Contact* (2010); *Foster Care and Social Networking* (2011); *Social Networking and You* (2011); and *Ten Top Tips on Supporting Education*, with Kate Cairns and Chris Stanway. In earlier collaborations with Kate Cairns, she co-wrote BAAF's training programmes: *Trauma and Recovery*; *Safer Caring*; *Building Identity*; and *Transitions and Endings*. Most recently she wrote two books in this series: *The Adopter's Handbook on Therapy* (2016) and *Caring for a Child who has been Sexually Exploited* (2018).

Introduction

Children spend on average over 7,800 hours of their life at school in the course of their education (OECD, 2014). At its best, school can be a place where young people learn to become all that they can be; it can open the doors to discovery, inspiration and friendship, as well as providing a well-rounded education that equips each child with the knowledge and skills they need for life. But it can also be a struggle, especially for those in care or adopted, when schools too often fail to meet children's learning needs and school life can be an ordeal for them.

As a parent, clearly your attitude to your child's education will go a long way towards shaping their expectations and aspirations and helping them to do as well as they can. Encouraging them and supporting them, sitting by their side and listening to them read, cheering on the sidelines when they're playing for the school football or netball team, helping them with homework, celebrating with them when they have tried hard or done well – these are all ways in which you will show your adopted child that you love them, that they are worthy of your time and care, that you think they are great, and that you want to help them learn. It will be a revelation for a child who has never had this before.

The school's approach, of course, is key when it comes to supporting children and young people who have experienced neglect and abuse (and those damaged even before birth) and who have different needs than those of their peers. They need understanding and extra support – sometimes a little, sometimes a lot – in order to simply cope with the demands of being at school, let alone to learn effectively.

Many adoptive parents say that they do not feel their children are being supported sufficiently at school. If a child is not enjoying it and is struggling, this is a source of stress not only for them but also for their worried parents.

This handbook is for you. By suggesting some of the things you need to know or do to support your child's education, it aims to help them have the best possible experience at school.

Much of the information and advice in this guide is likely to apply to children's experiences of school across the four countries of the UK. However, their educational systems vary. Scotland has its own regulatory structure, its own set of exams and curriculum, and a wider, more flexible approach. England, Wales and Northern Ireland are broadly similar with occasional discrepancies. This book makes reference to the framework in England, but much of the content will be useful throughout the UK.[1]

We begin with a look at the context – the current social and economic pressures on schools and child and adolescent mental health services (CAMHS), but also the positive impact of measures such as the Adoption Support Fund (ASF) and the extended roles of designated teachers and the virtual school. There follows a brief explanation of how a legacy of early traumatic and difficult attachment experiences may affect children's ability to cope with school life and learning. We go on to look at approaches that schools and teachers are using to support children, and how you, as a parent, can work with your child's school to help teachers and others understand his or her needs, as well as what you might be able to do to help your child cope with the demands of school. There are tips and case studies to help you navigate the system, including managing transitions to primary and secondary schools, working with teachers and accessing special needs support, plus a list of organisations and resources where you can get further information and support. An appendix provides some basic information about who's who in the education system and how it works.

The combination of positive experiences of education and school and a stable, loving home can turn a child's life around. In the words of Collette Isabel Bentley, adopted at 10 years old after troubled years in foster and residential homes:

> *Time and time again, my education was a vehicle through which my "parents" transmitted a crucial message: 'You are worthy of our love, care and expectations.' As a child who had been rejected and abused, humiliated and shamed, it was overwhelmingly invigorating to have an adult care enough to learn my French vocabulary with me ... to have an adult buy me an appropriate PE kit so I wouldn't have to face humiliation at school.*

(Bentley, 2013, pp. 51–52)

---

1 For more information about education in the devolved countries visit: www.learning.wales.gov.uk (Wales); https://education.gov.scot (Scotland); and www.deni.gov.uk (Northern Ireland).

There is still much that needs to improve in the English education system. Training teachers and having enough staff in schools depends on resources and schools are in a funding crisis. The services that should be supporting adoptive families also struggle at a time when local authority budgets are under severe strain. But with their adoptive parents to advocate for them, and with growing understanding among teachers, we hope that more and more adopted children will get the support they need and find school a safe and nurturing place where they can achieve everything they are capable of. There are some encouraging developments. A growing number of adoption support organisations, parents and other individuals with expertise in this area are working to get schools and teachers to understand the issues and change their classroom practices and behaviour management policies. An increasing number of schools are finding out how to get it right for adopted children and other young people who have had adverse early experiences.

Every child is unique. Every school is different. We know that a book like this can never address every question and there are no easy answers to many of the issues around adopted children and schools. Hopefully you will find things that make you reflect, or that spark ideas you could share with your child's teachers. Above all, we hope that it will help you to support your child to be able to enjoy school life and make the most of everything it offers.

1 Supporting adoptive children in school: the context

Children who have been adopted after a period of being in care (previously "looked after" in Government terminology) are now in a loving home with parents who will work hard to support their education. Many of them will make accelerated progress in school once they are settled, and go on to do very well. But it is recognised that some of these children are still likely to need extra help. The Government acknowledges that:

> Many looked after and previously looked after children have suffered disrupted learning, may have missed extended periods of school, and many of them have special educational needs (SEN). The gaps in their learning and, in many cases, the emotional impact of their experiences, are likely to have become significant barriers to their progress.

(Department for Education, 2018, p. 8)

and that:

> Looked after children and previously looked after children are more likely to experience the challenge of social, emotional and mental health issues than their peers. For example, they may struggle with executive functioning skills, forming trusting relationships, social skills, managing strong feelings (e.g. shame, sadness, anxiety and anger), sensory processing difficulties, foetal alcohol syndrome and coping with transitions and change. This can impact on their behaviour and education.

(As above, p. 25)

Pressures on schools

So it is recognised that many adopted children have additional needs in the classroom. However, teachers have a punishing workload and the demands on their time are huge. Most adoptive parents are only too well aware of the challenges teachers face in meeting the needs of all the children in their child's class, which is likely to include several who have special needs of one kind or another.

With austerity affecting school budgets as never before, accessing extra help or one-to-one support for children who need it is not always easy. Many schools and colleges are having to let go of teachers, teaching assistants and learning mentors because of budgetary pressures, which means children with additional needs do not always get the support they should have.

Local support services for children and families have been cut to the bone in many areas. This means that there are increasing demands on schools and teachers to deal with issues in families struggling with anything from debt to domestic violence which might, in the past, have been dealt with by other agencies.

A survey of school leaders in 2017 found that more than two-thirds said they lacked the support they needed to ensure that pupils with special educational needs and disabilities were achieving their potential (Evans, 2017). They criticised rigid assessments and the narrowness of the curriculum.

There is a huge emphasis on academic achievement in schools – which, of course, is as it should be. But it should not be to the exclusion of all other considerations, and definitely not if this means discouraging or even excluding children who are unable to reach the required standards.

Schools are still judged on their test results and league table positions, which puts huge pressure on head teachers and teachers, not to mention children and young people themselves. There have been claims and campaigns based on the belief that the amount of testing and exams imposed on children and young people is having damaging effects on their mental health. Many parents and teachers feel that the current testing regime is imposing unacceptable pressures on children; teachers may feel that they have to "teach to the test" and that children's curiosity is stifled.

Children's and young people's mental health services (CAMHS)

Children's and young people's mental health and the state of services for them are of huge concern to professionals, parents and children alike. In June 2017, then Health Minister Jeremy Hunt announced plans to train 3,000 secondary school teachers in England as mental health "first-aid champions" so that schools could identify and respond to early signs of mental illness in pupils. The scheme would be extended to primary schools, he said. However, by the end of 2017 almost two-thirds of secondary schools still did not have a dedicated mental health champion. Tristan Donovan writes:

> A survey of 603 school leaders and governors by Leeds Beckett University's Carnegie Centre of Excellence for Mental Health in Schools found that 65 per cent said there is still no dedicated staff member in their school who is trained in or given responsibility for pupils' mental health.

> The survey also found that 58 per cent felt there was insufficient mental health support available for school children, despite 83 per cent reporting rising levels of mental illness among pupils in the past five years.

> Almost every respondent (97 per cent) said mental health support in schools needs more funding and 93 per cent wanted more guidance on the issue from the Department for Education. In addition, 77 per cent wanted Ofsted school inspections to examine the quality of mental health provision.

> The findings follow the publication of a Government Green Paper earlier this month that set out plans to have a designated senior lead for mental health in every school, mental health support teams to work directly with schools, and reduced waiting times for accessing child CAMHS.

> Jonathan Glazzard, professor of teacher education at Leeds Beckett University, said:

> 'We welcome the proposals in the Government Green Paper, 'Transforming Children and Young People's Mental Health Provision', which was recently published.

> 'However, the proposals will be gradually rolled out over several years, so not all pupils will receive the support they desperately need. Our research

shows there is a clear need to address the issues of funding and training immediately.'

...The university's survey also found that school leaders are worried that internet and social media use is damaging children's mental health, with 86 per cent saying social media is having a detrimental impact on young people's lives and 89 per cent wishing parents would restrict the amount of time children spend online.

Last year, the Government said it would provide an extra £1.4 billion to improve CAMHS up to 2020, but there are concerns that clinical commissioning groups are diverting this money to other health services.

(Donovan, 2017)

CAMHS is notoriously overstretched. The Government has said it will introduce a four-week limit on waiting time for treatment but currently waiting lists are long and thresholds for eligibility for treatment are high (with some children being given the message that they are 'not sick enough to be seen'). Mental health professionals' understanding of adoption issues is sometimes lacking.

The Adoption Support Fund

Some adoptive families have been able to use the Adoption Support Fund (ASF) set up by the Government to provide a pot of money for therapeutic psychological support for adopted children and their families, to access expert assessments and specialised therapy, among other things. However, there is now a £5,000 cap on the fund for therapy in most individual cases, which means the support offered does not always go far enough. (In a few cases the local authority will be able and prepared to match-fund the cost of therapy over £5,000.)

The ASF currently excludes educational support. Some feel that education should be included in its remit:

Schools need help from adoption agencies to create a therapeutic approach to education for adopted children in mainstream schools...The Department for Education should consider funding therapeutic interventions in schools for adopted children as part of their review of the Adoption Support Fund.

(Alan Burnell, Registered Manager, Family Futures, 2017)

The role of designated teachers

There have been some encouraging recent developments in terms of support for adopted children in schools.

Designated teachers for looked after children are teachers within a school who have a special responsibility for promoting the educational achievement of children in the care system. As of 2018, their role has been extended so that they also cover previously looked after children, i.e. children adopted from care or under special guardianship.

They are expected to know about issues such as trauma, attachment difficulties, foetal alcohol spectrum disorders (FASD) and the kind of support adopted children may need.

Statutory advice from the Government lists the following issues for schools and designated teachers to consider:

- whether any looked after and previously looked after children have special educational needs (SEN) and whether those needs are being identified and met at the appropriate level;

- whether any looked after and previously looked after children have mental health needs and whether those needs are being identified and met;

- whether the school's behaviour management policy is sufficiently flexible to respond to looked after and previously looked after children's challenging behaviour in the most effective way for those children;

- how the teaching and learning needs of looked after and previously looked after children are reflected in school policies, in particular in relation to interventions and resources.

(Department for Education, 2018, p. 30)

In the case of adopted children, designated teachers are expected to involve the child's parents or guardians in decisions affecting their child's education, and be a contact for parents or guardians who want advice or have concerns about their child's progress at school.

So it is a good idea to get to know the designated teacher at your child's school from the very start, so that hopefully you can work together to bring about any adjustments or extra support your child may need.

Virtual schools

Virtual schools, set up to support the education of looked after children, also now have an expanded role and are tasked with providing information and advice for adoptive parents.

Virtual schools have statutory duties in respect of looked after children because the local authority acts as a "corporate parent" for children in the care system. A virtual school head (VSH) oversees the educational progress of all the looked after children in the local authority, even though they are in different schools. The virtual school is responsible for the allocation of the Pupil Premium for looked after children and for liaising with each school about the child's Personal Education Plan (PEP) (see Chapters 4 and 5).

When it comes to adoptive children and their families, the role of the virtual school is different because these children do not have the local authority as a corporate parent.

> *For previously looked after children, the VSHs are no longer acting as the part of their corporate parent: their role is limited to providing information and advice to parents and schools, including training to raise awareness and understanding of their needs. The designated teacher may, however, seek the advice of the VSH about meeting the needs of individual children with the agreement of the child's parents or guardians. It is, therefore, important that the designated teacher establishes a good working relationship with the VSH for their area.*

(Department for Education, 2018, p. 30)

The service each virtual school can provide may depend on the staffing and funding allocated to them by the local authority (see Appendix). Some provide training for teachers in issues around attachment and adoption. Some are able to offer a consultation service for schools where an individual child is having difficulties, put a support plan in place or help mediate where there is some conflict between the parents and the school.

Before going into details about what you, as an adoptive parent, can do, let's look at how your child's early experiences might affect their ability to cope with school life and readiness to learn. Many adoptive parents will be familiar with the concepts of developmental trauma, attachment difficulties and FASD. You will almost certainly have learned and read about these in preparation courses and post-adoption training; and many of you are living with the impact, every day, on your child and your family life and are only too well aware of the implications for school life and learning. However, it may be helpful to understand how such a history can specifically affect children's experiences of the school system.

Key points

- It is a challenging time for schools, mental health services and anyone who is concerned about the life chances of children with educational and mental health difficulties. Parents need to get all the support they can for their child, stay strong, mobilise and campaign – if they have the time and energy – and advocate for their child's needs.

- The ASF provides valuable funding for therapeutic psychological support but this has yet to apply to interventions in schools.

- Each school has its own designated teacher(s) in charge of promoting the education of looked after and adopted children. Their responsibilities include knowledge of the effects of trauma, attachment issues and FASD in order that they can identify needs and deliver the best possible targeted support.

- Every local authority in England has a virtual school overseen by a virtual school head (VSH) who is responsible for the welfare of looked after children in several schools. This role was recently expanded to provide information and advice for adoptive parents. How much VSHs will be able to deliver in face of a continuing shortfall in overall school funding remains to be seen.

2 How do early experiences affect children's ability to cope with school and readiness to learn?

The lives of adopted children, even when they are in a loving and caring adoptive family, continue to be profoundly affected by what happened to them early on. The neglect, abuse, chaotic environments and traumatic events that caused them to be removed from their birth families and the grief and loss of disrupted attachments can shape the way in which they see themselves, other people and the world around them. Children who have had a difficult start can be left with vulnerabilities and gaps in terms of their psychological and social development and their ability to regulate their emotions and behaviours.

A child may be highly intelligent but unable to do well at school – or sometimes even cope with school at all – because of emotional, social and behavioural difficulties that are the legacy of their early experiences. It's worrying and distressing for parents to see that their child is stressed or unhappy in school, falling behind his peers or struggling to make friends because of his difficulties in forming relationships, or because his unpredictable behaviour makes other children wary of him.

For some adopted children, damage was done before they were even born, when they were exposed to alcohol and/or drugs in the womb. Pre-natal exposure to alcohol, when a woman drinks during pregnancy, can damage the developing brain of the foetus. It can cause permanent neurological deficits, affecting the child's ability to concentrate, learn, remember and understand (see 'Understanding the effects of FASD').

The impact of trauma and attachment difficulties

We know that many adopted children did not get the warm, responsive, attuned parenting that builds secure attachments between babies and their parents or carers. When children are neglected and abused by their main caregiver(s), this affects their ability to form secure attachments. These early experiences can have a long-lasting impact on many aspects of a child's later development, including learning, emotions and social skills. For example, they may struggle to understand, express and control their emotions and may often feel unsafe, under stress or overwhelmed by feelings of shame even when they are in a loving adoptive family.

> Due to earlier trauma and disrupted attachment experiences and negative internal working models, children will often see themselves, others and their world through their trauma and insecure attachment mirror... 'I'm vulnerable', 'Others are dangerous', and 'The world is unsafe'. Therefore, although they may currently be in a "safe" school environment, this does not mean that they feel and believe that they are safe...and so we often see children's strongly developed defences/fight-flight-freeze at play within the school context.
>
> (Treisman, 2017, p. 149)

Repeated losses – being removed from the birth family home, being moved from foster carers – can leave them with unresolved grief and the constant fear that they will once again be taken away from everything they know. All adopted children will have experienced at least one disrupted or broken attachment. As a consequence, many adopted children develop an insecure attachment style: they relate to others in an anxious, avoidant, angry/ambivalent or disorganised way. They find it difficult to put their trust in adults, seek comfort, accept guidance, feel safe, make friends, empathise with others and to achieve many of the everyday things that come easily to other children.

Children cannot learn if they feel unsafe, if they cannot trust their teacher or if they are too afraid of rejection and failure to try and learn new things.

Building a new attachment with a child who is placed with you for adoption can take a long time. And at school, your child has to spend long periods of time away from you and share the teacher's attention with many other children. This can trigger his attachment needs or attachment-related trauma, as he wonders whether Mum/Dad will still be there when he gets home and whether they will have forgotten him.

Teachers are increasingly becoming aware of the importance of attachment, and children who used to be seen as "clingy, attention-seeking and disruptive" are now being recognised as "attachment-seeking".

Here are two short case studies showing how attachment difficulties can play out in the classroom:

> *Ten-year-old Amber... would regularly shout out in class and often follow the teacher around the room. Through a thorough assessment, it emerged that Amber had previously been starved of adult attention, and had been significantly neglected. She had learned various survival strategies for being kept in the minds of others; her shouting out was her way of communicating, 'Don't forget me, please remember me.'*

> *Five-year-old Dylan had experienced unavailable/absent parenting. He had learned to conceal, internalise and/or deny his emotions. Within the classroom this showed itself as Dylan being overly self-reliant and compliant. He avoided teacher support, seemingly from fear of being rejected or ignored. This, in turn, made him fall under the radar and appear "invisible", and once again mirrored his early experiences of being forgotten and neglected. This reinforced Dylan's insecure–avoidant attachment style and his expectations of being ignored, invisible and unimportant.*

> (Treisman, 2017, p. 148)

School requires children to trust adults and relinquish control to them – something that children who have experienced abuse at the hands of trusted adults can find particularly difficult to do. This can go against the defence mechanisms and "survival strategies" they may have developed in their birth families.

Children's difficulties also affect their relationships with other children. Sometimes their emotional and behavioural needs can make it hard for them to make and keep friends. If a child is withdrawn, or too controlling, is volatile and prone to lashing out or having meltdowns, has not learned to take turns and share, other children will be wary of them.

Feeling unsafe

The feeling of lack of safety described earlier can result in children becoming "hypervigilant" or "dissociating" at times of stress. When they feel unsafe (which may be much of the time while they are at school), children can be on high alert, constantly in "fight" mode and preoccupied with possible threats. This means that they may overreact to things such as someone touching them or appearing suddenly behind them, which can mean they "kick off" in the classroom and, if the teacher doesn't understand, can find themselves in trouble.

In other children, or at other times, the child "zones out", withdraws and becomes dissociated from everything going on around them. The teacher may interpret this as simply not paying attention, daydreaming, and so on.

Such children may even do certain things without realising consciously what they are doing, which again can get them into trouble.

Dysregulation

If babies have not been cared for by an adult who is attuned to their emotions, who is there to soothe them and help them calm when they are distressed, they will not develop the ability to reliably regulate their own emotions. They can quickly become overwhelmed by feelings of stress and fear (which may play out as anger).

Dysregulated behaviour can look different for every child. In the classroom it might mean fidgeting, making repetitive noises, calling out, chattering and giggling, lashing out, becoming withdrawn and even things like urinating somewhere inappropriate. A dysregulated child is liable to flare up, over-react to seemingly small things, or become overwhelmed in stressful situations. These behaviours, of course, often don't go down well in the classroom or with peers. Their impulsive, volatile behaviour can get them into trouble.

Dysregulated children need an adult to whom they are attached who can help them to regulate their emotions when they are feeling stressed, angry or upset. With help, as they grow older, children can develop some understanding of why they may struggle with their feelings and emotions. This 12-year-old adopted child describes it like this (with their own unique spellings!):

> *My brain works differently to other children and some of your sons or daughters brains will work the same as mine. So some of your children*

mite not no they need to think about other people feeling but children who haven't had so much trauma in there life will no you need to think about other peoples feelings as well as theirs. Some of your children will always think you are telling them off if you are saying 'Please don't do that.' But they are not doing it to make your life hard they think you are telling them off. Maybe some of your children when you are about to say something think you are going to tell them off even if you were going to tell them something nice. Lots of adopted children brains work like that so if they are shouting at you, are screaming or hitting or kicking, you still have to deal with it but never take it personally, they aren't doing it because they hate you they are doing it because they are angry. But half way through that meltdown they are sorry but they feel bad or embarrassed so they don't know how they say that so they try to get you drawn in so then they can say, 'But you did this,' so then this isn't on them. So the top tip in all of this is never take it personally.

(Anonymous, 2017)

Chronological age vs developmental age

Delays in children's development can mean that they feel, think and act much younger than they are. In school, adopted children often suffer because people's expectations are based on their chronological rather than their developmental age – and some are still operating at the emotional age of a toddler or much younger child:

They are often not developmentally mature enough to manage the requirements for independent goal-directed behaviours, impulse control, delay of gratification, anticipation of consequences and anticipation of their thoughts and feelings.

(Hughes, 2012, p. 37)

These children need teachers who understand this and can provide appropriate learning and play activities, supervision, boundaries and targets.

Executive functioning difficulties

Many adopted children experience difficulties with "executive functioning", namely the ability to organise, concentrate, set goals, plan tasks, process information, solve problems, switch focus from one task to another, and remember information and instructions. Problems with executive functioning can also make it more difficult for children to anticipate the consequences of their actions. It's easy to see how this makes school life and learning challenging for children. They may forget to bring into school the things they need, or have trouble concentrating or switching from one task to another, or find it hard to finish work in the time allowed.

Sensory issues and triggers

Developmental trauma affects the ability to process and integrate the information received from the senses – sights, sound, smell, touch, taste, body awareness and balance. Children may be unable to recognise when they are too cold, too warm, hungry or thirsty. Some are over-sensitive to sensory input and experience sensory overload in busy, bright and noisy classrooms. Certain smells and tastes can seem overpowering to them. Even their clothes may feel scratchy and uncomfortable.

When a child has sensory issues, the clamour of the classroom, crowds of children in the corridor, shouting in the playground and the queue in the dining hall can leave him feeling too stressed to function or even, sometimes, unwilling to go to school at all.

Negative expectations

The child may have spent his or her early years in a family where adults failed to attune to him or meet his needs or even left him isolated and rejected, which will have shaped his view of himself, others and the world around him. He may have internalised the notion of adults as intrinsically uncaring or hurtful, of the world as an unsafe place and of himself as a "bad child" who is worthless and deserves to be hurt. He may make negative assumptions about other people's motives.

In school, he may always expect to get things wrong, or to fail and may experience any mild form of instruction or correction as being told off or shouted at. He may expect rejection everywhere and believe that none of the other children like him, even if this isn't true.

In some cases, older children may also have absorbed the views of their birth parents that school is a waste of time, teachers are stupid, and there is no point in learning.

If we think we're in trouble it's going to make the situation a whole lot worse than it originally was...and then we just think it's going to happen all over again – we're going to be kicked out of school or something like that, because we always think we're at fault.

(Adopted young person speaking on a film produced by Coram Life Education)

Understanding the effects of FASD

FASD is a complex disability that is only recently becoming better understood in the UK. Children and indeed adults with FASD have a range of difficulties and will require some degree of support for life.

Many adopters may not have been aware, when they adopted, that their child was affected by FASD as this may not have been known at the time. More often now, children are being diagnosed before placement and adopters are given information about the condition – though it is still often not possible to know what the impact will be. Diagnostic services are patchy (see Mather, 2018, for an account of why diagnosis is so important). Even with a diagnosis and an awareness of the condition, supporting children with FASD in school can be a challenge for the child's teachers.

Just like children with relational trauma and attachment difficulties, some children with FASD may be bright but struggle to manage well in mainstream schools. The difficulties may not become apparent until the child starts school, or even later. Sometimes children do reasonably well in primary school but the complex demands of secondary education leave them unable to cope. They find any kind of change disruptive and destabilising.

They may hit a ceiling at Year 1, have big issues with transition to secondary schools, or their problems kick in at the start of the GCSE years. They need understanding, flexibility and realistic expectations.

(Brown, FASD Trust, personal communication)

Brian Roberts is head teacher of a virtual school and a trainer, and he and his wife are foster carers who took out special guardianship orders for a sibling group of three girls, all affected by FASD. He says the impact on a child's ability to learn is poorly understood, even by many people closely linked to their education. These children struggle to conform to the rules and social norms of school. Traditional learning strategies need to be amended to allow affected children to reach their full potential.

Roberts gives the following three examples of the challenges:

- *At the beginning of Year 11, a 15-year-old boy took a knife into his secondary school. He had picked up the knife when carpets were being fitted in his home and liked it so much that he wanted to show his friends. It was so important to him that he showed it to the first person he met at the school gate. Unfortunately, it was a Police Community Support Officer. The boy was permanently excluded, could not cope in the Pupil Referral Unit and at the end of Year 11 ended up with no qualifications. Most teachers would argue that this is not the typical behaviour of an adolescent who decided to take a knife into school. "Innocent delinquency" is the term often used to describe this type of behaviour, which is characteristic of the FASD child.*

- *An 11-year-old girl upset her maths teacher by "rudely" answering back in class in response to being told off for her behaviour and attitude. When the teacher attempted to quieten her by asking whether she thought the 'silly' comment she had made was funny, the "rude" answer was 'Yes, that's why I did it.' The child's reasoning was that the teacher had asked her a question and it would be rude not to answer and even ruder to lie...The FASD child frequently fails to understand adult sarcasm and often misinterprets everyday social communication.*

- *In nursery school, a three-year-old would scream and run away from the teaching assistant every time he saw her. This was after experiencing a whole day at nursery based on* The Gruffalo *children's story when the teaching assistant had dressed up as the Gruffalo. As a few of the younger children had been frightened, in order to reassure them the teaching assistant removed the costume's head. Most of the children were reassured except for this boy who was convinced that the teaching assistant was the Gruffalo. Distinguishing fantasy from reality can be a continuing struggle for the FASD child.*

(Roberts, 2015, p. 237)

It's important, as with all children, to see their strengths as well as their difficulties:

> *Students with FASD are often ambitious and have a range of practical strengths which are useful in their educational careers and throughout life.*

- *Many are articulate and have engaging personalities. They enjoy being with other people.*

- *Many have learning strengths around literacy and practical subjects, such as art, performing arts, sport, and technologies, although they often have difficulties with comprehension.*

- *While they have working/short-term memory difficulties, rote learning and long-term memory can be strengths.*

(NOFAS-UK, 2017)

NOFAS-UK (National Organisation for Foetal Alcohol Syndrome UK) has an excellent downloadable guide to help teachers to support learners affected by FASD in school, called *Teaching a Student with FASD* (see www.nofas-uk.org).

Difficulty in diagnosis

It may not be possible, or at least not early on, to get a firm diagnosis to explain the cause of a child's particular difficulties. The symptoms of many conditions can look a lot like each other. Diagnosis is not always straightforward.

To add to the difficulty, to get a diagnosis of a particular condition the assessment may need to be carried out by a particular specialist – for example, a paediatrician for attention deficit hyperactivity disorder (ADHD), an occupational therapist or sensory integration expert for sensory integration disorders, a speech and language therapist for communication problems, and an educational psychologist for other issues such as executive functioning problems and specific learning difficulties such as dyslexia and dyspraxia.

Getting your child's needs recognised, diagnosed and agreed by the various professionals and panels can be a long and challenging process. Some parents, faced with a long wait, resort to paying privately to have assessments done.

Traumatic stress in childhood seems to be linked to conditions like depression, anxiety, ADHD and conduct (behaviour) disorders. Children can also be subject to a range of other difficulties such as developmental delay, learning difficulty, speech and language issues and specific learning difficulties.

Some children show particularly extreme oppositional behaviour, which has been labelled "pathological demand avoidance" (PDA) – though some experts (and parents) are reluctant to apply diagnostic labels to children because of behaviour.

These children will go to any lengths to refuse to co-operate with adults and other children. They use a range of behaviours to avoid complying, ranging from passivity and refusing to speak, to manipulative behaviour and "kicking off" in public.

It's been suggested that PDA could be a type of autism but researchers are still not certain whether it is caused by some other disorder or is simply a separate entity that is often accompanied by other conditions. It's also not uncommon in children with language disorder and ADHD. Intervention and treatment are a challenge and currently largely a question of trial and error. Strategies developed for other conditions such as ASD and ADHD are often ineffective. Obviously it is extremely difficult for a child or young person with these difficulties to function in a mainstream school classroom.

Responding to needs, whatever the underlying cause

The child's intrauterine environment (if the mother drank alcohol and/or took drugs in pregnancy), genetic influences, early attachment experiences and adverse experiences in childhood all affect and contribute to the way a child functions and to the expression of disorders such as sensory processing difficulties, ADHD and depression. For example, children with attachment difficulties as well as those with FASD may be anxious about change and find it destabilising; become stressed and overwhelmed by aspects of school life; and find it less easy than their peers to form friendships with other children.

A diagnosis, if you can get one, can be helpful because it may well make it easier for everyone around the child to understand why he has these particular difficulties or behaves as he does. Hopefully it should also encourage teachers to have different expectations of the child and take the appropriate approach. But unfortunately it won't necessarily trigger access to support or therapy. The school should already be providing for the learning needs the child has, regardless of the cause.

In more severe cases of special educational needs and disability, a child who meets the threshold will have an Education, Health and Care Plan set up for them which outlines the extra support they should receive, or in some cases, the special school that they should attend (see Chapter 6).

In the following section we look at some of the strategies that can help children feel safe, secure and calm, whatever the underlying cause of their difficulties. We explore the ways in which teachers and schools can make the classrooms, school environment, teaching methods and behaviour policies and even some curriculum topics more sensitive to the needs of adopted children.

One size doesn't fit all. The teacher needs to get to know each individual child and be flexible and willing to adapt.

Key points

- Children's early experiences can have an enormous impact on their development, including their ability and readiness to learn. Teachers are beginning to understand this, in particular the role that attachment plays in how children cope with expressing and controlling their emotions, but there is still a long way to go.

- As an adoptive parent, you know your child best, so you will need to guide teachers about how best to help him feel safe and understood in the classroom.

- Children with early experiences of neglect or other abuse may feel, think and act much younger than they are. It is important that the school's expectations don't exceed your child's stage of development.

- Your child may have problems with "executive functioning", i.e. the ability to organise. Again, this needs to be recognised and understood.

- A significant proportion of adopted children are likely to have some degree of FASD resulting from their mothers having drunk alcohol in pregnancy. Diagnosis isn't easy but there are a growing number of resources to help you identify whether this might apply to your child and, if so, what it can mean (see list at the end of this book).

3 Approaches to supporting adopted children in school

The context described in the opening chapter is obviously concerning to teachers and parents alike, but there is a great deal of positive work going on in schools across the country. This chapter looks at some of the approaches and strategies that schools and teachers are starting to use to help "tune in" to children and support them.

As stated earlier, you will have already gained considerable knowledge about trauma and attachment through your adoption preparation, training and reading, as well as knowing your own child better than anyone else. You will need to draw on this knowledge when it comes to talking with your child's school and trying to raise awareness, or when you are visiting prospective schools if your child is approaching school age, or if you are thinking about changing school. (Chapter 5 goes into more detail about this.)

It's important to say that many adopted children don't necessarily need any special treatment or adjustments. They just get on with school, enjoy it and do well. But if schools can implement the approaches and strategies outlined here, there are benefits for *all* children, not only for those who face bigger challenges than their peers.

Building safety, self-regulation, trust and attachment

For children with developmental and relational trauma, feeling safe (at home and school) and developing attachment relationships (with their adoptive parents initially and then with teachers/school staff) are key to them feeling safe and able to learn in school. Of course, some children will also need treatment from therapists working together with you as the child's adopters in order to improve their emotional stability and achieve healthier attachments.

Many adoptive parents use the therapeutic parenting technique known as PLACE (playfulness, love, acceptance, curiosity and empathy) which aims to help the child feel safe and connected and to build stronger attachments. (For more information, see https://ddpnetwork.org/about-ddp/meant-pace/.)

This is part of a parenting model called Dyadic Developmental Parenting (DDP), which is taught in a type of family-based psychotherapy or in group workshops. DDP was developed by Dan Hughes, who set up the Dyadic Developmental Psychotherapy Institute in the US. (For more information, see www.ddpnetwork.org/parents-carers/.)

For a child to thrive in school, teachers as well as parents need to be able to behave in ways that will help the child feel safe and secure. "Playfulness" in a teacher can take the form of sharing fun and laughter in the classroom; "love" is about maintaining a loving attitude towards children who are not always easy to love; "acceptance" can mean accepting that the child's sometimes odd or challenging behaviours are not always under her conscious control. "Curiosity" means being interested in what makes the child tick – and perhaps wondering aloud: 'I'm wondering if this noise is bothering you?', or 'I'm guessing you are feeling upset because Mrs Kahn is not here today?'. "Empathy" means really trying to connect with the child and understand how it might feel to find everyday situations threatening and live in a constant state of stress.

Dr Bruce Perry, senior fellow of the Child Trauma Academy in the US, researches, writes and lectures about neuroscience and trauma, particularly how childhood trauma and neglect affect the brain's stress response systems. He developed the Neurosequential Model of Therapeutics (NMT), a theoretical framework for looking at how trauma influences development. He argues that in some children the lower brain, where intense emotions originate, needs to be regulated with the help of an adult. Once the child is feeling calmer, the adult can relate to the child emotionally; then the adult can help her to reason, i.e. to understand why she might have done what she did or how she might have done things differently.

Emotional regulation and dysregulation are terms that are now much more commonly used in education and psychology as well as within the adoption community.

Bruce Perry suggests that patterned, repetitive and rhythmic somatosensory activities such as music, dance, drumming, swinging and bouncing on a trampoline are good ways of reaching the dysregulated neural networks involved in the stress response. This knowledge and approach can be useful for teachers working with children who easily become dysregulated, as well as for parents.

Attempting to reason with or correct a child while she is in a highly aroused state of anger or distress will not work. What she needs is for an adult to first help her calm down and connect with her.

"Co-regulating" by an adult can eventually lead to the child developing the ability to self-regulate. They need to learn to recognise and identify her feelings and find ways to de-escalate when becoming stressed or angry.

Bruce Perry went on to develop the Neurosequential Model in Education, to look at how NMT can be applied in a classroom setting by school staff who have been taught what makes an optimal learning environment for a child with a history of trauma.

How does this work in practice? It's still early days for this approach but in 2016, in a small-scale qualitative study of four teachers using NME in Canada, it was found that:

> *The NME model increased teacher, educational assistant and student knowledge about the brain, brain development and the impact trauma has on the brain, and provided tools to help with student self-regulation, preparing the classroom atmosphere for improved learning.*

(Walter, 2016)

Some of the tools used were "brain/regulation breaks"; making a "mini-map" of the functioning of a child (looking at things like reactivity/impulsivity, self-regulation and attention/distractibility); heart-rate monitors to help students build awareness of their heart rate during difficult situations; and having students write a journal every day to reflect on what made them worry, what made them upset, and what made them feel better, to help them become more aware of their feelings and triggers and how to cope.

> *Participants used the NME classroom management tool "Regulate>Relate>Reason" to respond to student challenges by providing regulatory opportunities first, then relating to the student, and finally reasoning with the student.*

(Walter, 2016)

There is no one single therapeutic technique or practice that will address all the complex needs of traumatised children at all stages of their development. But thanks to experts like Dan Hughes, Bruce Perry and others who are writing and providing training in the UK, together with the work of organisations such as PAC-UK and Adoption UK, among others, there is a growing body of knowledge about approaches and strategies that parents and teachers find helpful.

A framework for schools is developing

Under pressure from Ofsted inspections and school league tables, some head teachers feel as though they have to choose between being a high-achieving school that emphasises high academic standards, and a nurturing school that welcomes and values children of all abilities. However, others maintain that a more nurturing environment actually helps children achieve as well as make them happier. They point out that if children are stressed, they cannot learn – so supporting them to feel safe and nurtured helps remove barriers to their learning and raises achievement across the school; and what is more, a whole-school nurturing approach benefits all children, not just those who are adopted.

Until recently, there has been little in the way of a framework for schools to support children with emotional, cognitive, social, behavioural and learning needs stemming from their pre-natal or early life experiences. Thankfully, that gap is now starting to be addressed.

The message is getting through that "difficult" or "challenging" behaviours that some children show in the classroom or playground are an expression of their feelings of stress, fear, anxiety and being overwhelmed by emotions they cannot control. There is a growing realisation that traditional sanctions and methods of managing behaviour in the classroom may not work with traumatised children, and an increasing readiness to adapt to their individual needs.

Many teachers are becoming more aware of things that might trigger anxiety, panic, overwhelming emotions or distressing memories in an adopted child; they are becoming more thoughtful about the curriculum topics that might make a child feel "different" or singled out because they are adopted. This is thanks to the work of many individuals, organisations and institutions – and, crucially, adopted children and young people and their parents.

Experts such as Louise Michelle Bomber, Dr Jennifer Nock, Kate Cairns, Dr Karen Treisman and others, adoption support organisations such as PAC-UK and Adoption UK, educationalists (e.g. at Bath Spa University) and organisations such as the Nurture Group Network are leading the way in introducing these concepts to schools and teachers. (For more details, see the Useful Resources section towards the end of this book.)

- Peer support groups such as NOFAS-UK (a support organisation for anyone affected by FASD) produce resources to explain how teachers can help affected children to realise their potential.

- In addition, adoption agencies are increasingly making education part of their adoption support. There is more collaborative working between adoption services, virtual schools and educational psychology services.

- The Government recognises the additional needs of adopted children with initiatives such as Pupil Premium Plus, priority admissions to schools for adopted children, extending the role of virtual schools to include providing information and advice to parents of adopted children, and extending the designated teacher role in schools.

"Attachment-Aware Schools" and "Adoption-Friendly Schools" (see Useful resources) are programmes that provide training, support and recognition for schools that are doing the right things. With whole-school training and sometimes consultation with experts, school staff can come to understand the underlying reasons for children's behaviour; to recognise that tried and tested teaching methods and behaviour management systems may have limited or no success with children who have trauma-related and attachment difficulties or FASD; and to adopt a different approach that promotes feelings of safety and emphasises nurturing and relationships. In these schools, head teachers, teachers and other school staff are making adjustments in their schools, classrooms, teaching styles and pastoral support systems in order to help mitigate the challenges that school life can pose for adopted children.

Evaluating attachment-awareness work

Many people are convinced that all this work is having good results. The Rees Centre for Research in Fostering and Education (University of Oxford Department for Education) has recently evaluated "attachment awareness" work in schools in Bath & North East Somerset and Leicestershire. It summarised the evaluation findings like this:

Most participants commented positively on the impact that the programme had had on their own attitudes, practice and confidence. The quality of training was reported to be a major factor in this.

Participants described changes in their practice, in particular recognising emotions while managing behaviours, changing communication styles and language used with pupils and other staff and, for nearly all the participants, use of emotion coaching.

School staff and pupils described the school environment as having become calmer and more nurturing.

Staff and pupils gave examples of non-teaching staff's positive responses and effective approaches.

Impact on pupils' well-being was evidenced by staff and pupils. One factor contributing to this seemed to be providing spaces in which children can calm down and self-regulate, another was having a significant adult in school that the pupil trusted.

Senior leader commitment, support and resource allocation was crucial to effective engagement in the programme and it having an impact on the school.

(Rees Centre for Research in Fostering and Education, 2018)

To further strengthen the evidence base for this kind of work, the Rees Centre has also set up the Alex Timpson Attachment and Trauma Programme in Schools, a five-year programme of research that will look at at least 300 schools in approximately 20 to 30 local authorities.

The aims of the programme are to:

- *raise school staff awareness and increase understanding of the role of attachment and trauma in children's education and strategies to better address their needs;*

- *reduce exclusions from school and improve attendance of children who are vulnerable;*

- *improve educational progress and the well-being of children who are vulnerable;*
- *develop the confidence and skills of teachers and other staff (including early years) to address trauma and attachment;*
- *identify the most effective approaches to addressing attachment and trauma in schools;*
- *build a strong national evidence base for schools and others, including national policy-makers, to draw upon in making decisions and allocating resources.*

(Rees Centre for Research in Fostering and Education, 2017)

Attachment figures and having a "key person"

Building trust and attachment can be difficult for class teachers when they do not have much time with the child every day and they have limited time to give one-to-one attention. Nonetheless, it is important for a child to have the opportunity to build attachment with one or two "safe" adults in school: this may be the teacher, a learning assistant, key worker, or someone else who acts as a mentor and attachment figure.

As explained above, one of the key things an attachment figure can do is what Dan Hughes calls "connection before correction". In other words, connecting emotionally with the child, acknowledging their feelings and showing you empathise with them before you attempt to model the desired behaviour.

Some schools identify a key member of staff for a child who has difficulties regulating their emotions, such as a mentor or teaching assistant (see 'Helping a child who is becoming dysregulated', below).

Together with the child, the school identifies a person in school who is well placed to regulate that child and how they will do it. That person is sent for if the child is, for instance, having an angry outburst or a panic attack in the classroom. The key person will ideally get to know and understand the child well, build trust, anticipate the child's needs and difficulties and advocate for the child within the school. In time, they may be able to help the child develop her reflective skills, emotional literacy and social skills.

Children can see their key person every morning when they arrive at school, or at breaktime or at the end of the school day, so they can discuss anything that is making them worried, upset or angry. The key person is someone who will provide one-to-one attention, listen and care when things are not going well, celebrate when things do go well, and acknowledge the challenges for the child. They may, for example, play turn-taking or trust games, or there might be a "bucket" where the child can metaphorically put people or things she doesn't like or is worried about.

Here's an example:

> *Seven-year-old Dante regularly had outbursts in both the classroom and at lunchtime. Through a process of really getting alongside Dante...and together with the support of attachment-informed consultation sessions, his teaching assistant was able to find several strategies that were effective in reducing incidents and increasing positive moments. Some of these included: having a personalised sensory box; starting the morning with drumming sessions; having a zen-zone filled with items such as weighted blankets and bubbles; using picture checklists; and having outdoor brain breaks.*
>
> (Treisman, 2017, p. 156)

Feeling safe in the classroom

The following considerations are important when helping a child who is experiencing stress, anxiety and fear:

● Teachers need to keep an orderly classroom environment as far as possible.

● They need to project calmness themselves, avoiding shouting (which a previously abused child could perceive as threatening).

● They also need to understand what, for this particular child, is likely to provoke anxiety, shame or distress. The trigger might be a particular sanction (or even a reward), changes, surprises, excitement, a school trip, unstructured time or something that sparks a memory of a traumatic incident. Children who are anxious and find friendships difficult can dread break times. Teachers need to understand the child and make adjustments.

● Most children enjoy the pre-Christmas period at school, when the usual routine is often left behind in favour of special Christmas-related activities and treats. But a child who struggles with change can find this slightly chaotic period in school very stressful, so teachers need to be mindful of this.

- If a child is hypervigilant and cannot concentrate because of anxiety, it may help if the teacher allows her to choose where to sit in the classroom. For example, the child may feel safer if she is sitting close to the teacher or may prefer to sit with her back to the wall where she can see the classroom door, so that she is not stressed by the thought of people coming up behind her.

- Perhaps the most important thing that helps the child feel safe in the classroom is knowing that the teacher "gets" her and understands her difficulties. There are ways that parents can work with the teacher to help with this (see Chapters 3 and 5).

Helping a child who is becoming dysregulated

In addition to the points above, some other things that can help a dysregulated child in school are listed below. Each child is different, so it's a question of knowing what works for an individual child:

- a "safe corner" in the classroom or school to retreat to (described below);
- physical effort, e.g. digging, scrubbing;
- activity such as jumping on a trampoline;
- playing with play dough, fidget spinners, etc;
- putting a blanket over the child (there are specially weighted blankets available for this purpose);
- bubble machines;
- rocking chairs;
- music;
- stress balls;
- drumming sessions;
- "brain breaks" – for free time, to play a game or move around – to allow the brain time to process information;

- time outside, e.g. walking or running round the school field or playground.

A "safe corner"

An important way of helping a child to calm down is to provide a physical safe place with a sense of safety, calmness and containment – this can be a sensory room, a pop-up tent or a special corner set up with cushions, blankets and other things that can have a calming effect on children, such as those above.

Ideally, a child should have a way of letting the teacher know when she needs to go to a special place where she feels safe, when the classroom or playground environment feels too overwhelming or threatening. Not all children will recognise when they need to do this, so the teacher/teaching assistant needs to be sufficiently tuned into the child's emotional state to recognise when she needs to be taken there. Older children and young people may be able to recognise for themselves when they need to retreat for a while and should have permission to leave the classroom if necessary to calm down. Some schools have been willing to set up a system for a particular child to notify the teacher that she needs to go there, such as showing a special card.

Recognising behaviour as "communication"

He carries the trauma with him very profoundly every second of the day and that's what we struggle to make people understand.

(Adoptive parent, personal communication)

Biting, hitting, kicking, shouting, swearing, running out of the classroom... For a teacher attempting to teach a class of 30 children, a child who disrupts lessons in this way can make teaching pretty much impossible.

A different approach is needed, which starts with understanding why the child is behaving as she does.

Teachers need to know how to manage such behaviour – for the sake of the child, for the sake of the rest of the class, and for their own sake, because the child is clearly under extreme stress and it can also cause great stress for the teacher and other children who have to deal with it every school day.

Nicola Marshall is an adoptive mother of three teenagers and founder of BraveHeart Education. She explains the need for flexibility:

> Probably the hardest and most important area for schools to address is our obsession with modifying behaviour. What we have at the moment are systems that essentially work on the premise that children and young people have the same level of respect for authority that they used to have and, indeed, that they all have the same understanding as each other and the ability to change their behaviour when we tell them to.

> Zone boards, sticker charts, marble jars, sun and dark clouds, house points, incentive schemes, yellow and red cards, isolations, detentions, time outs and exclusions all rely on a child's ability to join the dots between their behaviour and the consequences. If I know that when I speed in my car I might kill someone and end up in prison, does it stop me speeding? It should, and most of the time it does, but there are odd occasions when I forget, or maybe my anxiety over being late, or whatever it might be, takes over and drives my behaviour to ignore the rules.

> Children and young people who've not had the chance to develop cause and effect thinking and may be operating in the survival part of their brain cannot manage their behaviour just because we move them down the zone board or show them a red card. In fact, for some children, being "on a red" gets them the most attention and that's what they most crave. They need someone to notice that they are struggling and to keep them safe.

> Moving away from these punitive, shame-riddled systems will take time and can be messy. We have to concentrate on relationships and understanding the child's experience of school. We may even have to change our approach to certain children, when we consider what their early experiences might have been like.

> (Marshall, 2018)

Successfully managing behaviour in children with emotional, social and behavioural difficulties requires teachers and other school staff to understand something about the impact of trauma on the brain, to see behaviour as "communication" and to develop strategies for successful intervention that are based on the importance of attachment, warm and empathic relationships and increasing the child's feelings of safety and decreasing their feelings of anxiety.

Children who may have been deprived of affection and/or harshly punished in early life for getting things wrong are liable to experience an overwhelming sense of humiliation and shame when they are told off (even mildly) or singled out from the rest of the class.

Some schools arrange training for all school staff – teachers, teaching assistants, kitchen and serving staff, office and caretaking staff and after-school providers – so that increasingly all the adults in the school begin to look at "challenging" behaviour in a different way. Rather than seeing it as naughtiness, silliness or the child trying to wind them up, they begin to see it as behaviour that the child cannot help, as a sign that the child is dysregulated, or as a throwback to their days of surviving in a dysfunctional family. When this type of training is successful, people are more willing to be flexible and to adopt alternative approaches.

Teachers need to get to know the child in order to get beneath the behaviour and reflect on what is actually going on for him or her, what the message is and what hidden emotions are behind the behaviour. Obviously parents are the ones best placed to help teachers to "get" their son or daughter, so by working with the school you can help bring about change. Teachers then have the opportunity to use more appropriate responses.

Emotional awareness

Children's early adverse experiences can affect their ability to identify, understand and manage their own emotions and to empathise with other people's feelings.

Schools are adopting a wide range of initiatives and interventions that aim to build children's emotional literacy. For example, one approach is called "emotion coaching":

Emotion coaching was first introduced by John Gottman and his colleagues in the USA. Emotion coaching is about helping children to become more aware of their emotions and to manage their own feelings, particularly during instances of misbehaviour. It entails validating children's emotions, setting limits where appropriate and problem-solving with the child to develop more effective behavioural strategies.

In effect, emotion coaching techniques instil the tools that will aid children's ability to self-regulate their emotions and behaviour. It enables practitioners to create an ethos of positive learning behaviour and to have the confidence to de-escalate situations when behaviour is challenging. Emotion coaching provides a value-added dimension to behaviour management strategies and creates opportunities for longer-term solutions to children's well-being and resilience.

(www.bathspa.ac.uk/education/research/emotion-coaching/)

Emotion coaching has the potential to help many children, but those more seriously affected by trauma will need more targeted support such as therapy.

Sensory issues

Schools and teachers need to be ready to make adjustments for children with sensory issues.

- As explained earlier, the school or class teacher can set up a "calm area" or cosy nurture room to which the child can withdraw to when feeling overwhelmed. Some schools already have such special spaces for students with autism.

- Children who are bothered by noise may find it helpful to wearing noise-blocking headphones.

- Some children may need to sit somewhere away from the lights or windows if they find it too bright.

- Those who find the feel of certain items of the school uniform unpleasant might need permission to wear something different.

- Other adjustments might include the child being able to do tasks that help her to avoid the playground at break time, if that is overwhelming for her, or allowing her to eat her lunch somewhere other than the school dining hall.

Every child is unique, and each child will need different adjustments in order to feel comfortable in school or to work well in the classroom. Below is one adopter's account of some of the measures that made a difference for her son, whom she refers to as 'Little Bear'.

'I feel hopeful now'

A couple of weeks ago I blogged about how Little Bear was doing at school, the apparent desire to keep us at arm's length and my concerns about the school's ability to support and educate him. Little Bear's behaviour was spiralling and his teacher was tearing her hair out. It was going badly and I was very worried. Since then I have had several conversations with his teacher, parents' evening and we finally had the big meeting we had been asking for.

The landscape now is very different. I think they are getting more right than they are getting wrong and Little Bear is starting to thrive. I thought it might be helpful to share some of the things we/they have done that have made the difference.

A timetable

Don't ask me why but when Little Bear started Year 1 there was no set timetable of what he would be doing each day; sometimes it could be maths then literacy, at other times phonics then maths, etc. His teacher realised after a few weeks that he might cope better if the expectations were clearer and his day was more predictable. They created a timetable for him but things were still going awry. I wondered aloud one day whether Little Bear was able to see the timetable himself. It turned out they were showing him the black and white typed adult version which was of course entirely meaningless to him.

Little Bear now has a timetable made up of digital photos of him doing all the different tasks. This is working fabulously.

He knows the routine and seems much happier to get on with what he is meant to be doing. Plus he actually likes the timetable because he is in it and is therefore much more motivated to engage with it.

"Choose" time

As Little Bear finds it difficult to concentrate for any length of time, we agreed that he would do alternate short work tasks with "fun tasks" to keep him on track. The fun task would be used as a carrot in a "now work, then fun task" kind of way. The fun task might also involve moving about to give him a physical/sensory break from sitting still. The fun tasks have been chosen carefully so they are still educational (they might involve developing his play skills or turn-taking or creativity, etc) and are actually motivating to Little Bear, not just perceived to be motivating by an adult.

The choices are presented to Little Bear in photo form (with him in the pictures) and he picks in advance of each work activity.

This is also working brilliantly to the point where some mornings he is now able to complete all the work tasks on his timetable and doesn't need any fun tasks at all.

A consistent approach

None of the above would be working if it wasn't for this. The teacher and teaching assistant (TA) have now figured out their strategy and are being much clearer with Little Bear. There is no shouting one minute then letting him off with something the next any more. I think they have settled on a calm, firm approach much like we use at home.

They have also realised that Little Bear benefits from some extra rules where other children wouldn't. For example, if he is tired one day and therefore allowed to read just one page instead of three, he will expect that he can do the same thing the next day. If he can find a chink in the armour he will exploit it. However, if there is a blanket rule such as "every day we read three pages", Little Bear knows where he is at and is much happier to adhere to it.

I think his TA was feeling mean about doing this but has found out the hard way that Little Bear actually feels a lot safer when he knows exactly what is expected and adults around him are consistent with their boundaries. If not, his anxiety will spike and his behaviour will become increasingly challenging. Now that he feels safer, he is much more open to learning.

A discipline re-think

The school as a whole were using the "Good To Be Green" behaviour system, which involves children getting an amber warning card when they do something they shouldn't and then a red card if they do something else, or do something violent. Thankfully they did see early on that this didn't work for Little Bear. There are the immediate issues with public shaming but for him the main problem was that once you get an amber or red card you can't work your way back to green that day. Once you've got in some bother and already had a red card, what is the point of trying to control yourself for the rest of the day? You might as well just go for it and do whatever you like.

It is a very negative system. Also, Little Bear was getting upset by the card changes because he isn't naughty, he just finds controlling himself really difficult. He was frequently very annoyed with himself for seemingly having failed, which impacted his mood for the rest of the day.

Thankfully school recognised that they couldn't continue with that system for him so came up with a new system, "Magic 1,2,3", to use instead. They didn't want to single Little Bear out with his peers so have changed the system for the whole of his class – a very sensitive gesture, I felt.

I'm not sure that I love "Magic 1,2,3" per se but it has an accidental benefit which is crucial for Little Bear. Basically, the teacher counts each time you do something you shouldn't, so you get three chances to make amends or make a different choice. If after three chances you still haven't co-operated or you have had three separate misdemeanours, you have to sit on the "thinking chair".

Now, I know a lot of parents won't like it because it is basically sitting in the corner. However, for Little Bear it gives him the calm-down time he desperately needs.

I have struggled to get school to understand that when Little Bear is thoroughly pissed off, the last thing he needs is someone lecturing him, talking at him. He needs to sit somewhere quietly until he is ready to talk. At home, we just ask him to sit wherever he is. He sits on the floor and we stay nearby and usually he'll say, 'I'm ready, Mummy,' after about three seconds (a "time-in"). However, it turns out that school weren't ever allowing him this time, so it wasn't any wonder he was nearly blowing a gasket sometimes and going straight from one incident to another.

Sitting on the "thinking chair" gives him just the de-compression he needs. Also, it is in the classroom so he is not isolated or left alone.

I don't think this would be the right thing for every child but it is suiting Little Bear much better and his behaviour has calmed enormously.

Praise and positive reinforcement

Little Bear's behaviour was becoming such an issue in school that I felt all the positives were getting lost. They had pretty much got to the point of thinking there weren't any. Apart from me pointing this out, I don't really know what changed, but the teacher and TA have certainly got better at looking for the positives and making a big fuss about them.

Again, this wouldn't work for children who can't handle praise but Little Bear really thrives off it. School have cottoned on to this and whenever Little Bear tries hard or produces something good, they encourage him to share it with the class. He absolutely loves this and I think it helps his peers to see him as someone who is successful, not just someone they think is naughty.

Working as a team

I do feel that school have recognised that they had cut us out of the loop and are now keen to include us more. I think they can see the benefits and that when there are meetings it is not because we want to tell them off or be difficult, it is because we genuinely want to work in partnership. We have two further meetings arranged, which has allayed a lot of my concerns.

We have agreed common goals such as to extend Little Bear's reading from three pages to four in one sitting and to encourage him to work independently for two minutes instead of one. The goals are achievable and measurable which is exactly as they should be and because we are working on them at home and at school I'm sure they will be met more quickly.

A key part of the meeting we had was to share information about Little Bear's history with his new TA. She didn't know how long he had been with us, what his developmental starting point was, etc. It would have been much more helpful for her to know all this at the start because then she could have adjusted her expectations accordingly from the outset. However, we can't undo the past and at least she is now armed with all the facts.

Communication

To help school to communicate with us in a way that works for us, they invited us to have a discussion and be clear about what we actually want to know. We have agreed that they will comment on Little Bear's behaviour each day and how he has got on with his independent working, hopefully in a 'one thing that went well and perhaps a thing that didn't go so well' sort of way.

Lateral thinking

School have been great about being open to different ideas and ways of doing things. Sometimes they still struggle to get Little Bear to have a go at things; he might flatly refuse or say he hates whatever it is. They have agreed to try things like offering Little Bear the opportunity to go and show his brother his work if he tries hard at it. I think he will be extremely motivated to do that and Big Bear is happy to be involved and relishes the added responsibility.

As the TA directly asked us for some advice on how to manage this, we were also able to talk about wondering and empathising, for example: 'It must be hard to get your work done if you hate English. I wonder if that's because you find it tricky' rather than a dismissive, 'You don't hate it.'

It meant more to us than they probably realised to be asked and to be considered a source of knowledge about our child. The head teacher also apologised to us and admitted they had got the transition badly wrong. He asked what could be done differently next time.

We left the meeting feeling reassured, listened to and that Little Bear is in safe hands. They might not get it right all the time but at least they know that and are not afraid to admit it and ask for help.

I feel hopeful now.

(Blogfox14, 2017)

Encouraging friendships

More and more schools are addressing children's social difficulties and recognising the need to promote kind and caring behaviour, to encourage children's friendships and tackle bullying.

Some of their approaches include:

- nurture groups;
- a buddy system, where the teacher puts in place special friends or friendship groups for children who are new to the school or who are struggling to make friends;

- peer mentors – often children from higher years in the school who can work with younger ones to encourage friendships or to give them someone to talk to if they are worried or upset;

- playground games organised by trained lunchtime supervisors to help children make friends, to provide structure at breaktime and to reduce conflict in the playground;

- lunchtime and after-school clubs for Lego, ICT (information and communications technology), Pokemon, etc, so that vulnerable students have genuine options for somewhere to go if they don't like the playground or the football field or if they find it easier to interact with other children over a structured activity.

When your child has formed some friendships, it is important to "cultivate" them by ensuring they have the opportunity for playdates, tea after school, etc.

(Karen Wilkins, adoptive mother)

Recognising trauma triggers and sensitive issues in the curriculum

Common curriculum areas that adoptive parents often mention as tricky for their children are: being asked to bring in pictures of the child as a baby (which you may not have); writing about your early life; assemblies about maltreated children (e.g. by the NSPCC); and being asked to draw a family tree.

In secondary school, for example, discussion around genetics, such as 'What colour eyes do your parents have and what colour are yours?' can enhance an adopted child's feeling of being different from peers who are not adopted. Lessons about drugs and alcohol can stir up unhappy memories of birth relatives misusing these and also make a child worry about developing the same problems. Sex education lessons could be uncomfortable or upsetting for a child who was sexually abused in early life, as could lessons about the effect of alcohol in pregnancy, for young people with FASD.

I've had the NSPCC come to school...and they were talking all about kids being abused and neglected and I was quite young but it hit me really hard – like – wait, I've actually been abused and neglected...I went home crying and crying to my mum because I could not understand what had happened. But if my mum had been told beforehand the NSPCC were coming into school and they're going to talk about this, she would have been able to tell me the information I needed to know instead of me finding out then going home crying and not understanding anything.

(Adopted young person speaking on a film produced by Coram Life Education)

If teachers know about these triggers they can try to help your child avoid them in the classroom. So, as a parent you will need to make the school aware (although not necessarily give all the details) so that they can make some adjustments (see Chapter 5).

Schools need to be aware of how the curriculum can trigger questions for adopted children. Our school consults adopters and foster carers before they show any of the sex education-type videos. Incidentally, I do believe there is an opportunity to provide schools with an adoption-friendly version of this! The video our school uses is very dated and does not reflect the diversity of families in modern Britain. Quotes such as, 'We all come from our mummy's tummy' can be very confusing for an adopted child who knows they didn't come from their mum's tummy.

(Karen Wilkins, adoptive mother)

As explained in Chapter 2, children who have missed out on early nurturing experiences may be delayed in their emotional development and have the needs and behaviour of a much younger child. So it is helpful for the teacher to adjust expectations and use approaches targeted to the child's emotional age rather than his actual chronological age.

Helping a child with executive functioning difficulties

For a child who struggles to organise herself, remember things, follow instructions and manage tasks, these approaches can help:

- Having a mentor/one-to-one time with a member of the school staff at the start and end of the school day or with whom she can "check in" at certain points to make sure she has all she needs, has understood homework tasks, knows where to go next, and so on.

- When giving instructions to the child, the teacher can use the child's name first, to get her attention; then give precise, rather than general instructions, such as 'Emily, go to the changing room and put on your gym kit and trainers' rather than just 'Get ready for gym.'

- Tasks should be broken down into manageable chunks to help the child understand how to tackle them.

- The school can keep spare gym kits, pencil cases and so on for children who have forgotten to bring their own.

- Visual timetables at home and school, which show the child in pictures and with simple words what she needs to do and at what time (e.g. getting ready for school) or what exactly will be the sequence of events on that day in school. (The pictures on the visual timetable can even be photographs of the child doing the various activities, which will help give her ownership and help them relate to it.)

- Together with your child, you can help by getting her school clothes and school bag ready every evening so that they are there for her in the morning, with no last-minute panics. Get her into a routine of packing her bag and checking off a list of all the things she needs to take each day (consulting the visual timetable).

- Help your child with time management of homework, prioritising urgent tasks but ensuring that she doesn't forget the less urgent tasks.

Celebrating success

Some children are very fearful of making mistakes because they have learned in their early life that doing something wrong will incur an adult's anger or punishment. Fear of making mistakes can lead to children being unable to take part in classroom activities; they are too anxious that they will fail.

Finding something they are good at can really help. If they do not excel in the classroom, they may enjoy music or school sport, or joining a choir or out-of-school activity or club such as swimming, Brownies or Scouts, or keeping a pet. Anything out of school that helps build their self-esteem will have a knock-on effect in school too.

The teacher can give your child tasks that she can do in the classroom to build a sense of achievement:

- Set the child up to succeed. Give her tasks that you know she can do, so she can build on these small successes.

- Reassure the child that making mistakes is just part of learning.

- Praise her for trying.

- Ask her to help the teacher.

- Ask her to help a younger child.

Some children find praise hard to take, so it needs to be chosen and delivered with care. If a child cannot accept praise or sabotages attempts to reward her, you (and the teacher) need to find other ways to do it – for example, praise what she has done rather than praising the child herself: 'That little boy was so pleased when you shared the Lego with him' rather than 'You are a good girl.' Praising in private might be easier for the child rather than in front of everyone, and praising in non-verbal ways with a high-five or pat on the back can work well. Being specific is also good: 'I like the way you have used those bright colours in your picture' rather than simply: 'That's lovely.'

Adoption advocates/designated person

As part of PAC-UK's project work with schools in London, an established network of "adoption advocates" is now facilitated by the schools themselves and is being widened to schools that did not participate in the project. These advocates can act as the key link between home and school. They get to know the adoptive parents and act as a mediator between parents and school. Parents feel as though they have a voice in the school and the child or young person can be confident that the adoption advocate will be there for her in school.

This role is likely to be increasingly taken by the "designated person" for adopted children in each school.

One school's journey to becoming attachment-friendly

Jennifer Nock is a chartered psychologist and educator who has worked for over 30 years in a wide range of education and special educational needs settings, with educators, children and young people, families and fostering and adoption agencies.

Writing in *SEN Magazine*, she described how one school put into practice its resolve to provide effective, lasting support to pupils with attachment issues. The school was Hope School in Liverpool, a Key Stage 1, 2 and 3 school for boys with social, emotional and mental health difficulties. The head teacher wanted to explore a more nurturing approach to behaviour than the traditional reward and sanctions-type methods that the school was using at that time.

Over the following several months, the senior leadership team (SLT) developed a strategic plan to improve attachment-friendly practice. Initial training on attachment and trauma was delivered to the whole staff, including the leadership team. The SLT looked at what staff were doing currently and how they might change their behaviour management methods:

> *The SLT prioritised developing adult calmness, self-control and modelling appropriate behaviour. They also advised that staff avoid getting into tit-for-tat exchanges with pupils, and reduce any interactions that raised children's stress levels, as these often back pupils into a corner from which they cannot escape. Instead, staff were asked to offer two good choices, for example: 'Would you like me to sit with you, or are you better on your own?' Staff were asked to give instructions in a calm and positive manner, where phrases like, 'Don't get the Lego on the floor' become 'Keep the Lego on the table, please'; 'Don't get stressed!' becomes 'Deep breaths and slow breathing'. Staff were also asked to increase the use of proximity [e.g. having the pupil sit near them], the pupil's name and frequent firm, respectful touch, as these often have a calming and grounding effect on dysregulated pupils. Four pupils were identified to receive an intensive intervention, including the allocation of key workers to support each of the pupils.*
>
> *For each boy, a targeted programme of intervention included a daily meet-and-greet session on entry to school, a daily relationship-based play session with the key worker and a sensory and body work programme. Individual interventions included a weekly sand tray session, use of calm box activities*

when early signs of over-arousal were observed, daily massage and emotional literacy games and activities.

(Nock, undated)

Key points

- There's a growing awareness of why some adopted children struggle with school. Understanding where a child's difficulties come from is the first step towards being able to offer the right kind of support.

- Professionals in the fields of trauma, attachment and FASD, academics, adoption support organisations and adoptive parents are working hard to get the message through to schools and teachers across the country so that they can make the adjustments children need and support them to achieve all they are capable of.

- "Attachment-Aware Schools" and "Adoption-Friendly Schools" are programmes developed to provide training, support and recognition for schools that are taking the challenges on board.

- The more that you, as an adoptive parent, know and understand about your child's needs and behaviour, and the techniques that work for her, the more you will be able to help guide the school.

4 Choosing and starting a new primary school

When is the best time to start school?

Children in England generally start school in the September after their fourth birthday. However, the compulsory age for starting school is five. A child reaches compulsory school age on the "prescribed day" following his or her fifth birthday. The prescribed days are 31 December, 31 March and 31 August.

According to the Department for Education's School Admissions Code:

Admission authorities must provide for the admission of all children in the September following their fourth birthday. The authority must make it clear in their arrangements that, where they have offered a child a place at a school:

a) *that child is entitled to a full-time place in the September following their fourth birthday;*

b) *the child's parents can defer the date their child is admitted to the school until later in the school year but not beyond the point at which they reach compulsory school age and not beyond the beginning of the final term of the school year for which it was made; and*

c) *where the parents wish, children may attend part-time until later in the school year but not beyond the point at which they reach compulsory school age.*

Admission of children outside their normal age group

Parents may seek a place for their child outside of their normal age group, for example, if the child is gifted and talented or has experienced problems such as ill health. In addition, the parents of a summer born child may choose not to send that child to school until the September following their fifth birthday and may request that they are admitted out of their normal age group – to Reception rather than Year 1. Admission authorities must make clear in their admission arrangements the process for requesting admission out of the normal age group.

Admission authorities must make decisions on the basis of the circumstances of each case and in the best interests of the child concerned. This will include taking account of the parent's views; information about the child's academic, social and emotional development; where relevant, their medical history and the views of a medical professional; whether they have previously been educated out of their normal age group; and whether they may naturally have fallen into a lower age group if it were not for being born prematurely. They must also take into account the views of the head teacher of the school concerned. When informing a parent of their decision on the year group the child should be admitted to, the admission authority must set out clearly the reasons for their decision.

(Department for Education, 2014b, pp. 24–25)

The advice above is in the School Admissions Code for admissions authorities, local authorities, school governing bodies, etc.

The advice for parents on school admissions (given on the Government website) is shown below – with no mention of children starting outside their normal age group (i.e. in Reception rather than going straight into Year 1):

Delaying when your child starts primary school

You can ask for your child to be held back a school year if the following both apply:

- *they were born in the summer (1 April to 31 August)*
- *you don't think they're ready to start in the September after they turn four*

They could start school in the September after their fifth birthday.

Contact the school's admission authority to make a request. This is usually the school or local council.

(www.gov.uk/schools-admissions/applying)

Schools cannot compel parents to send their child into school under the compulsory school age (five). However, at the moment the admission authorities can make the decision on whether a child starting school at five must go straight into Year 1 and miss out on the Reception year.

The Summer Born Campaign (www.summerbornchildren.org) is campaigning so that summer-born children can automatically be admitted to Reception at compulsory school age so that they do not miss out on that important year of early education. Some parents whose children were born prematurely also feel that their children should be allowed to start in Reception at five rather than four.

The Department for Education has this advice for parents:

> ... whilst evidence shows that, statistically speaking, summer-born children tend to perform less well in school tests, this does not mean that all children born in the summer term will struggle at school. Teachers are skilled at differentiating the curriculum to meet a diverse range of needs. Before deciding to delay their child's entry to school, we would recommend that parents visit the schools they are thinking of applying for. The teachers will be able to explain the provision on offer to children in the reception class, how it is tailored to meet the needs of the youngest pupils and how the needs of these pupils will continue to be met as they move up through the school. They may also be able to allay any concerns the parent may have about their child's readiness for school.

> It is also important to note that, whether they attend a primary school or an early years setting during the academic year following their fourth birthday, children will receive the Early Years Foundation Stage curriculum which is largely based around learning through play.

> (Department for Education, 2014a)

Many adoptive parents also feel that their children need extra time at home to catch up on developmental stages they may have missed.

Schools Minister Nick Gibb said in early 2018 that ministers will instigate a change to the admissions system to ensure that all summer-born children have the option of starting in Reception at age five. Unfortunately he did not say when this change would happen, only that it would be "when the opportunity arises" – and he first promised it in 2015. No further progress has been made since then.

Here is some advice for adoptive parents from virtual school head, Michael Bettencourt:

This is a grey area that the Government did not legislate on for summer-born children and there is nothing adoption-specific. Most admissions authorities should have a policy or guidance but each situation is dealt with on a case-by-case basis.

My advice to adopters would be this: you can request that your child is educated in a year group below their chronological age, but please note it is a "request". Make sure you put the request in writing and be prepared to provide evidence relating to all aspects of your child's development. I would suggest that it needs to be more than simply preferring your child to wait a year or feeling that they are not ready.

The evidence you refer to could include:

- *the views of the head teacher (if he/she is in favour of your request);*

- *medical reports;*

- *the views of your adoption worker;*

- *reference to national research on summer-born children;*

- *reference to national research on adopted children; for instance, see* Becoming an Adoption-Friendly School *by Emma Gore Langton and Katherine Boy (2017), one of the few publications that has evidence on education outcomes of adopted children.*

Other sources of evidence could be reports from the Virtual School Head and/or a clinical or educational psychologist – basically anyone who has worked with the child or can provide a view on their development.

Further things to think about include:

- *Adopters may have to request this directly from schools that are their own admissions authority (e.g. faith schools).*

- *At times of transition the issue may crop up again, so in Years 2, 6 and 11 the request may theoretically need to be made again, particularly if the child moves schools or areas. If the request was denied then the child would have to go back to their chronological age cohort (it's not likely but worth being aware of).*

- *Your child could theoretically leave school early, e.g. in the middle of A levels.*

(Michael Bettencourt, Virtual School Head for South Tyneside Council and Research Lead for the National Association of Virtual School Heads, personal communication)

So a "postcode lottery" continues and parents must fight their case with admissions authorities at a local level. Some manage to get agreement for their child to start at five, rather than four, in Reception. Other parents are not presented with the option.

We didn't feel Cameron was really ready (she had just turned four and was still very young and not interested in learning her letters or numbers). But we discussed this with school when we did a tour around and they pointed out the disadvantage late starters can have in terms of forming positive relationships. They accepted she was a young four-year-old but said that she would benefit from the friendships at school and this would build her confidence. When children join school six months or a year later, they have missed that early period in Reception year where friendships are first developing and this can make them feel more isolated.

(Karen Wilkins, adoptive mother)

Starting school in a pre-adoptive placement

When your child is about to move in with you in a pre-adoptive placement, you are likely to have to choose a new school for him (if he is of school age).

Cambridgeshire Virtual School has produced the following information sheet for schools, with advice on how all parties can prepare for the child starting a new school and ease the transition for the child. It says the primary concern in a pre-adoptive placement is for the child to develop relationships with the new family. The child needs to feel safe and secure. This is likely to mean a short period when he is not in education. The aim of its advice is to minimise the impact that this may have on the child's progress and attainment, as well as to ensure a smooth transition into the new school. Cambridgeshire Virtual School points out that the appropriateness of the strategies below should be considered in light of each child, family and school's unique situation.

Before the child moves in with the pre-adoptive family

- *The choice of destination school should be discussed with the virtual school.*

- *The prospective adopters should organise to visit the possible schools to look around; the virtual school may be able to support these visits. The schools should provide the prospective adopters with a prospectus and any other relevant documentation. This is an opportunity to find out about the school's experience of supporting children who have experienced early trauma or have attachment needs.*

- *Once a collective decision has been made about the most appropriate school, the child's social worker is responsible for completing and submitting the admission form.*

- *It may be appropriate for the family to visit the existing school to meet with the teacher or designated teacher to get a flavour of the child's learning profile. This would be in addition to the school being invited to attend the child appreciation event. However, it is likely that the child will be unaware of the match at this point. Therefore this may need to be after school hours, or alternatively if there is a time during the day when the child is not on the school site, so that the child does not inadvertently come into contact with the prospective adopters.*

- *A transition meeting should be held that includes the current school and new school, current carers, prospective adopters and virtual school. This should focus on the current school's and carers' experience of what works well, both in terms of supporting the child's emotional needs and educational progress. It should detail transition arrangements with rough timescales for visits and starting school. It will be possible to alter these at any stage, but having them in place early can minimise drift.*

It is important that everyone has a common understanding of names used by the child, when talking to and about their adoptive and birth families. Consideration should be given to the surname by which the child will be known (this could be either the birth or adoptive family name).

- *The current school should consider appropriate leaving arrangements, e.g. peers to make cards, possibly purchasing a book that the class have focused on as a gift, leavers' assembly. The child's "key adult" will be especially important, leading up to the change of placement and school. The school needs to be receptive to the fact that the child may need additional reassurance and "nurture time" while also recognising the need for consistency and routine. It may be appropriate to have an age-appropriate, direct conversation with the child along the lines of: 'You may have a wobble, this will be hard but everyone is going to help you settle and do your best.'*

- *The current school should ensure that they collect photos, work, videos, etc. of the child's time at school, which can form part of their life story work.*

Once the child has moved in with the pre-adoptive family but before starting at the new school

- *The pre-adoptive family could look at the new school website with the child and consider any questions that the child may have about the school.*

- *Organise a visit with the child to look around the school and ask any questions that they may have. The transition meeting should have given the new school an opportunity to find out about the child's interests, e.g. if the child is keen on sport, the tour of the school could incorporate a focus on the sporting resources and provision on offer within the school.*

- *It may be appropriate for the school to prepare a book for the child, with photos of key adults and areas of the school, to share at home. It may be possible to organise for the child to take home a class teddy, which they could bring back to school when they start. For an older child, it may be helpful for the class teacher to create an "all about me" sheet for the child to have. This can help the child to quickly feel more comfortable with the teacher.*

- *The school can provide the family with information on the themes/topics that are being covered and ideas of how the family could support pre-learning, ready for when the child starts school. This may include experiences and active learning, e.g. if the theme is autumn:*

  - *go to the local park;*

  - *play in the leaves;*

  - *collect leaves for a collage;*

  - *take photos of autumnal things, e.g. conkers, bare trees, etc;*

  - *create prints or leaf rubbings;*

  - *sort leaves by colour, size, shape;*

- visit the library and get non-fiction books on autumn and related story books to share at home;

- carry out internet research on the seasons.

The purpose of immersing the child in these sorts of activities is to enable bonding with the family and familiarity with the local environment, as well as exposure to vocabulary and experiences that should help the child feel that they have valuable contributions to make when they start school. It may be appropriate for the child to bring into school some of the things that they have completed at home to share with their teacher/key person when they starts school. It is important that there is no stress or pressure associated with the activities; you will need to judge how much and which activities are most appropriate to your child and family.

To be in place for when the child starts the new school

- *Actions discussed at the transition meeting should be in place.*

- *The new school should consider organising a "buddy" to be with the child in the first few days.*

- *The child should have a key adult/s who will "touch base" with them regularly.*

- *Schools should bear in mind that "suddenly becoming parents" could mean that parents may have missed out on the events and experiences that many birth parents will have had, such as developing friendships with other parents in the community through antenatal classes, attending play groups or new parents meetings at school, where they have been exposed to approaches to early learning. It may be appropriate for the class teacher or relevant member of staff to meet with the parents to explain how the school approaches reading, phonics, writing, maths, etc. and how the parents can best support learning at home. Parents will also need information on general school rules and routines. You may welcome school support in meeting other parents and becoming part of the community.*

- *Schools should consider how best to develop home/school communication; parents may have lots of questions to begin with and will also need effective communication as to how their child is settling in.*

- *A PEP (Personal Education Plan) must be completed within 20 days of a school move (as the child is still, at this point, a "looked after child").*

(Reproduced with permission from Cambridgeshire Virtual School)

Choosing a school

Adopted and looked after children have the highest priority when it comes to school admissions, so your child should certainly be offered a place in whatever school you choose (apart from selective schools).

Choosing the right school to meet your child's needs isn't always an easy decision. The previous chapters will have helped to give you an idea of the kind of things schools and teachers can do to make school life better for adopted children.

Arrange a meeting with the head teacher of the school you are considering for your child so you can explain the issues he might have and the kind of behaviours the teacher might see. Be upfront about any difficulties so the school can work out whether it will be able to manage him. If it baulks at this first stage, then you will know it is not the right place for your child.

PAC-UK has identified some key questions to ask schools when you visit them. Below are the ones to ask primary schools. Many of the points apply to both primary and secondary (such as questions about the use of the Pupil Premium Plus), but of course secondary schools will have different ways of approaching things (see Chapter 6).

Key questions for primary schools

Parents often tell us that they don't know what to look for when choosing a school. In consultations with experienced adoptive parents, we've identified some key questions for parents and schools to consider. Not all will be relevant for every child. It's unlikely that any school will be doing all of these; look for flexible schools that are willing to listen and learn and are proactive about developing support to meet each child's needs.

Have staff received training on attachment and the impact of early trauma and loss?

Who was involved in the training?

For example:

- *Did senior leadership attend?*
- *Were teaching assistants included?*

- *Was it cascaded to playground supervisors?*

- *What has been the impact throughout the school?*

How does the school provide consistent key relationships for children with attachment needs?

For example:

- *named members of staff as key workers for children, with quality one-to-one time scheduled into the child's day or week, with particular attention to the times when the child is most vulnerable;*

- *staff who are aware of how to let the child know that they are held in mind;*

- *ways to help children stay connected, e.g. a postcard in the holidays?*

Where is the safe base for children when they need to calm down or regulate?

- *Is there a nurture group and how do they prioritise children to be part of this?*

- *Is it used as a planned daily intervention?*

- *Is there a nurture space or calming zone which children can access as and when needed with a key member of staff?*

What is the behaviour management policy?

- *Does the school apply the policy flexibly to best meet the needs of each child, e.g. if they use a yellow/red card system or a "sunshine–storm clouds" system for moving children "up" and "down" based on their behaviour, will they use a different non-shaming strategy for your child?*

- *Does the school see behaviour as communication and focus on meeting those needs?*

- *What is the school's approach to exclusion?*

What support is in place for children who find unstructured times difficult?

For example:

- *Is there an indoor lunch club for more vulnerable children, where they can develop their social skills, or calm down and relax?*

- *Do the midday supervisors organise structured games in the playground?*
- *Are there systems for children who want to play with friends, e.g. a buddy system or a friendship bench?*

How does the school provide structure and consistency?

For example:

- *sticking to the timetable at Christmas and ends of terms;*
- *letting parents and children know as soon as possible about staff changes and supply teachers;*
- *providing a schedule for parents to prepare the child at home;*
- *using visual timetables to let children know about upcoming changes.*

How does the school share the information you give them about your child's background and needs?

For example:

- *systems;*
- *meetings, policies, etc;*
- *If this is on a "need to know" basis, how is this decided and clarified with everyone, including parents?*

How does the school share information with parents?

For example:

- *Does the class teacher speak to parents at the end of the day, or call home?*
- *Are staff able to email parents if needed?*
- *Is there a text message system, e.g. to notify parents about snow days?*

How does the school connect adoptive parents and special guardians together?

- *Do they provide a coffee morning?*
- *Are they willing to have a standing item in their newsletter letting everyone know about any meetings convened by parents themselves?*

How has the school used its Pupil Premium Plus for adopted and special guardianship pupils?

- *Social and emotional interventions or only learning?*

- *Is the Pupil Premium Plus clearly differentiated from the overall pupil premium pot for children entitled to free school meals?*

- *Does the school meet with parents to identify children's needs (e.g. PEP meetings) or consult adoptive parents as a group about use of the grant?*

How does the school support children who find it difficult to manage their feelings?

For example:

- *nurture group;*

- *calm boxes;*

- *a calming zone within the school;*

- *emotion regulation skills teaching and coaching;*

- *anger management training;*

- *empathy from all staff;*

- *social skills groups.*

How does the school manage curriculum hotspots, i.e. issues that might trigger your child?

For example:

- *liaise with parents about baby photos and family trees;*

- *cards for Mother's and Father's Day;*

- *subjects such as evacuees in the Second World War in English and history;*

- *NSPCC and Children in Need assemblies.*

(Reproduced with permission from PAC-UK)

Even if the school is not doing everything it could be – and let's face it, few schools are perfect – you may be able to work with it to help the staff understand your child. With luck, if the school is open to listening, you may be able to collaborate with certain key members of staff to bring about changes in the school's approach that will benefit your child and other children as well. Read below how one adoptive parent encouraged her child's school to become more attachment-aware and adoption-friendly:

'Our big adoption-friendly/adoption-aware school choice gamble'

I don't buy lottery tickets or gamble, but when my husband gave me the responsibility of selecting our adopted daughter's school, that's exactly what I did.

Almost three years ago, while in the throes of building a family relationship and surviving instant parenting of a one-year-old and three-year-old, we were pressured by our children's social worker to select and apply for our daughter's school place fairly early into our placement.

Under time pressure, not knowing many local families with school-aged children and being fairly emotionally exhausted, I will admit to doing fairly limited local research – visiting one school. Excluding many of the immediate local faith school options, I grasped onto a neighbour's recommendation of a nearby free school. It had only been open for two years so came with many risks but it sounded amazing. After looking at reviews and reading about the school I applied, assuming that being a London school, they would have some experience of the needs of looked after and previously looked after children. I was sold on the sound of the nurturing but classic education offered with firm behaviour expectations. To be honest, I didn't even visit the school until the place was allocated.

So how have we got on?

Our daughter's school place was confirmed and I waited for the school to get in touch and arrange a home visit. When it became apparent this was not going to happen, I contacted the school, only to have doubts well and truly set in. They no longer offered home visits and could not have been less interested in allowing my daughter to visit the school to help prepare her for the move. This, along with the bad attitude of the (then) head teacher, left me spending the summer regretting the school choice and feeling like the worst parent ever.

Our daughter's first few weeks starting school were a test for me. She loved it immediately. I got five minutes on her first day to help settle her in the class and then had to leave her to it…. And it was so hard to leave. There were tears – mine! My assumption that the school would be experienced with understanding and meeting the needs of children with developmental trauma and compromised attachments was fairly misguided. Thankfully her teacher, despite being newly qualified, was incredibly nurturing and willing to learn and understand. Yes, some mistakes were made; for example, seating a distracted hypervigilant child with her back to the door, and not anticipating that changes of staff, environment or school trips lead to edgy/ hypervigilant behaviour.

Collecting my daughter at the end of the day was a lucky dip of either a food-angry, emotional daughter who could fly easily into aggressive tantrums and rages or a delightfully happy little girl, loving school and wanting to share every moment. My lowest point was sobbing in the SENCO's [Special Educational Needs Co-ordinator] office about the tantrums and self-destructive behaviours that started about the time our daughter started the school. She would hit herself in frustration or give herself massive nosebleeds, sometimes nightly, as a result of emotional anxiety, and consequently many mornings she and her bed looked like there had been a massacre. I learnt to come to pick her up armed with pockets full of snacks and not to expect a hello or hug until at least half had been quickly consumed.

While I had conflicted feelings about the school's lack of attachment experience/awareness, my daughter was thriving. The teachers were fabulous, the curriculum was amazing, and being a new "free school", the parents wanted to make it a success. There were many, many positives. Changing schools was not an option we would consider, as it would be further disruption. Speaking to other adoptive parents in the borough who had placed their children in schools known to be experienced with adopted children, I realised we were not alone in having challenges, regardless of the school's experience.

I decided that I would become an annoying squeaky wheel and "encourage" the school to work on becoming attachment-aware and transparent regarding how the Pupil Premium grant was spent. Luckily, the head teacher left at the end of our daughter's first term in Reception and a SENCO started. New staff arrived and it was a breath of fresh air. On a mission, I contacted and met with the interim head. After offloading, and then meeting with the SENCO laying out all the issues, the school was thankfully receptive to working with me on ensuring our daughter's needs were met and receptive to feedback on areas of improvement needed.

Our daughter now gets drama/play therapy sessions weekly and consistent staff to support her with changes. I'm notified in advance of changes so I can prepare her, she has access to confidence-boosting clubs/activities and is thriving. The school remains receptive to feedback and ideas, taking on board anything I feel our daughter might benefit from at school. They have started arranging regular follow-up sessions with parents of children needing support and are working on encouraging parents and carers of previously looked after children to meet up and support each other. Despite the odd tantrum and nosebleed, it's remarkable to reflect on how much more settled our daughter is and how excited she is to be returning to school shortly in Year 2.

As our son prepares to join his big sister and start school in a few weeks, I'm reminded of how far we have come! What a lovely feeling it is, this time round, to know he will be in good hands with a school that has observed him at nursery, had him do visits to the class and meet his new teacher, and provided him with a book of photos of the class/school/teachers to look at over the summer. His teacher is coming to visit at home and there will be a phased starting-school plan with clear parent/school communication to ensure his needs will be met. Nurture spaces are in place and support is evident. Staff have had attachment training and, once he settles, there will be discussion on how his Pupil Premium grant can be used to support him.

It is really nice to appreciate how far the school has come in two years. I took it upon myself to share with the school any information I came across regarding talks or training opportunities for schools, especially the free ones. I would follow up and repeat if needed. Thankfully, a deputy head and the SENCO have embraced the school working to become an attachment-friendly school, with the full support of the head teacher and governors. They have gone to great efforts to attend talks, become actively involved with virtual schools and more. Most important, they are working in partnership with parents such as myself on ensuring that the school understands and works towards meeting the needs of their looked after and previously looked after students.

So far, thankfully, the gamble is paying off. Perhaps it's time to buy that lottery ticket ....

(This blog has been included with the permission of We are Family, a network of adopters that runs four regular local groups in and around Greater London. On We Are Family's blog, members take turns to tell a story from their lives as families. For more information, see: www.wearefamilyadoption.wordpress.com.)

Special schools for children with special educational needs

Inclusion is a good aim but it's also important to look at the needs of each individual child to see if the mainstream school is meeting or can meet them. Mainstream school is not the best option for every child. The question of whether a child goes to a mainstream school or a special school can be a difficult and emotionally charged decision for parents.

Sometimes it is clear-cut but in other cases it may gradually become evident that mainstream school is not the right place for a particular child, even with all the extra support the school can provide.

Special schools with pupils aged 11 and older can specialise in one of the four areas of special educational needs:

- communication and interaction;
- cognition and learning;
- social, emotional and mental health;
- sensory and physical needs.

Schools can further specialise within these categories to reflect the special needs they help with, for example, autistic spectrum disorders, visual impairment, or speech, language and communication needs (SLCN).

If your child has an Education, Health and Care Plan (EHCP) (see Chapter 6) that specifies a certain school, that school must offer your child a place.

Special schools can provide smaller classes, teachers who are trained and experienced with pupils with special needs, and a peer group in which a child with difficulties will not stand out for the wrong reasons – because all the children face their own challenges. A special school is likely to provide a more nurturing environment where children are not defined by their difference, and their qualities and strengths in a wider range of areas are recognised and celebrated.

However, if it is decided that a special school would be best for your child, you may find that there is not much choice. Provision of special schools remains scant, especially for children with moderate learning difficulties and autism.

> *Independent special schools will often have superior facilities and resources such as in-house therapists, and they will more often specialise in a condition. County special schools can be a jack-of-all-trades, dealing with a wide range of conditions, and therapy provision can be scant (relying on visiting NHS professionals who will be severely overstretched).*

> *You need to investigate each school's pupil cohort. Are there some children of similar ability, even if they are different ages? (Special schools usually teach in ability groups rather than strict age groups.) Is there a good range of extracurricular activities?*

> *Of course the price tag for the independent specialists is usually significantly higher, so choosing one can require you to prove that it is the only suitable provision through a stressful tribunal. And don't be swayed by a local authority telling you your child should go to mainstream [school]. It's easy to see this as a signal that everything will work out, and your child's needs are not as severe as you feared, but remember that mainstream is the default option for local authorities, and they are likely to have pound signs rather than your child's best interest front of mind.*

> (John, 2017, p. 77)

(For organisations offering help and advice to parents of children with special needs, again see the section on EHCPs, Chapter 6.)

Starting school as an adopted child

Below are some suggestions for ways in which you can help prepare your child for starting school, or starting at a new school:

- Visit the school with your child before he starts, taking photos of the school and staff, making a book or photo album together about the school.

- Visit the school on quiet days and busy days.

- In some schools, the Reception year teacher visits children at home before they start school. Ask the teacher if you can take a photo of her/him for your child.

- You could even make a recording of the new teacher's voice so your child can become familiar with it before starting school.

- An introduction to the safe spaces at school can be part of the transition tour for prospective new students who are vulnerable in some way.

- With your child's input, put together an 'all about me' profile to give to his school and teachers – this will reassure the child, to some extent, that the teachers and school "know" him and understand some of the challenges he has.

- Explain the school policies and rules clearly, in a way your child can understand.

- Practise tasks your child may have to do at school with role-play so that he will feel more in control when the event actually happens.

- If you don't feel your child can cope with a full week of school, ask the head teacher if it would be possible for him to start with a four-day week instead.

Key points

- Your child does not need to start full-time school at four if you feel he o isn't ready.

- Choosing the right school for your child means assessing how ready the staff are to learn from you about your child and how flexible they might be about accommodating his needs in a thoughtful way.

- There are a number of ways in which you and the school can support your child when he first starts school.

- For children with special educational needs, mainstream school may seem desirable but it may not be the best option. Special schools have the advantages of smaller classes, trained staff and a more nurturing environment.

5 Working with your child's school and teachers

We have said it before and we'll say it again: you are the expert on your child. But sometimes parents lack confidence when it comes to speaking with education professionals. We hope this chapter will be useful in helping you think how to work with your child's school.

Interaction between home and school

School is a huge part of your child's life and of course it impacts on how she feels about herself and everything she does. For adoptive parents, it can be a joy to see your son or daughter wake up in the mornings looking forward to the school day, having fun with their friends, mastering new skills, developing new interests and growing in confidence.

But if things are a struggle for your child at school you are likely to bear the brunt of her feelings at home. Some adoptive parents report that their child has to make a huge effort at school all day to bottle up her feelings and cope with the stress of the classroom, school work, the playground and relationships with other children – only for her emotions to explode as soon as she gets to the safety of home.

She also has to cope with the power of the internet and social networking. These days, children as young as toddlers are watching content on tablets and mobile phones, with some people concerned about the possible long-term impact on their well-being. Many primary-school age children bring smartphones to school. (The effects of this – and especially the risks posed by social networking – are discussed at the end of Chapter 7.)

If discipline in the school is poor, with students' behaviour barely controlled and teachers under stress, this can make any child feel unsafe and anxious, and of course the impact of this environment will be greater on some children than others. If a teacher is sarcastic or shouts a lot in the classroom, this can adversely affect all the children in the class but again, the impact may be greater on a more vulnerable child.

Parents often have to deal with the fall-out of an environment that is not right for their child at school. Sometimes a child can have angry and destructive meltdowns; at other times it might be tears and sleepless nights. Of course, there may well be anger, tears and sleepless nights for parents themselves in these situations.

For some children, it is the other way around – they seem fine at home but they cannot manage their feelings, emotions and behaviour while they are in school.

All sorts of things both in and out of school can affect a child's ability to learn and to manage at school. For example, adopted children might have a lot going on in their heads that their parents are unaware of, because the child doesn't talk about it. A child may be constantly thinking and worrying about the welfare of birth family members or contact with birth relatives; she may have unresolved anger and questions about her adoption; she may fear not being "good enough" or feel that she doesn't belong in her adoptive family.

Talk to your child to try and find out what is going on for her and if anything is worrying or frightening her, either related to school or anything else in her life. Find ways to help your child express what is going on for her. Discuss your concerns with teachers. Seek outside help if necessary, for example, from your post-adoption support worker. Perhaps your child might benefit from some sessions with a play therapist, drama or art therapist to help her express her feelings and worries. You may want to involve the VSH in meetings with the school when you discuss how your child's behaviour should best be managed. With luck, between you all, you may be able to support your child through her difficulties and get her to a better place.

Finding some out-of-school activities that your child enjoys will help with her overall confidence and self-esteem, which will have knock-on effects in school too. If she can join a group like the Woodcraft Folk, Scouts, a cadet group, a dance class, sports club or band, for example, she may be able to have positive experiences and form new friendships there that will go some way to counteract negative experiences in the classroom and playground. If she can develop her skills and talents – and be respected within the group for it – this can help your child to feel better about herself, which will build her resilience.

Education Plan for Adopted Children

Some schools set up individual support plans for adopted children along the lines of a Personal Education Plan (PEP), recognising that they are likely to have some of the same needs as they did when they were looked after children.

Looked after children all have a PEP, to ensure that teachers and others come together to discuss their progress and what support they might need in terms of their education. This is a statutory requirement.

In the case of adopted children, the plan is not statutory and relies on the adoptive parents telling the school that their child is adopted. It may be called something like an Education Plan for Adopted Children (EPAC) or an educational support plan.

You, as a parent, can ask for this or the school may suggest it, either when you adopt a school-aged child or when your adopted child starts at a new school. This will establish ongoing regular reviews of your child's progress at school and planning for the future. How regularly meetings happen will be decided by the people at the EPAC meetings. For example, it might be three-monthly, six-monthly or once a year. The EPAC meetings will involve a member of the school staff (probably the designated teacher), other teachers such as the child's class teacher, the parent(s) and other professionals involved with the child. You may choose to invite, for example, your post-adoption support worker, at least at the beginning (see the comment below). Someone from the virtual school may also be able to attend.

The meetings look at the child's learning and development, strengths and needs, upcoming activities such as school trips, potentially sensitive curriculum topics, transitions, communication between home and school and any other information, including things that the child finds difficult and where he or she would benefit from extra support.

The meetings will decide on actions to be taken by the adults around the child to support her in or out of school, such as ways to help her cope with playtimes or lunchtimes and any special arrangements that might be needed for tests or exams.

The EPAC meetings are also a good time to discuss the use of the Pupil Premium Plus (PPP) (explained below).

It is essential for a member of the post-adoption team (or virtual school) to attend the first EPAC meeting with you. It adds a professional voice to the meeting, not only focusing on an individual child but can also lead to wider discussions about how adopted children's needs are met within the school.

(Karen Wilkins, adoptive mother)

The role of the virtual school and setting up a support plan

The role of the virtual school in respect of adopted children (rather than looked after children) is likely to vary depending on local resources, but in Cambridgeshire, for example, it is currently able to support adoptive families on an individual basis in meetings with the school.

At the moment, if families and schools make contact with us we can offer advice and guidance over the phone, but if it's quite a complex situation, then we go in and support meetings and set up the use of a support plan.

We call it an Education Support Plan. We try to distinguish it from the PEP because obviously it isn't a statutory requirement. We do observations and things like that when necessary. As this becomes more known about, the need for that will increase and increase and it's going to depend on the capacity we have got as to how much of that direct work we can do.

(Claire Hiorns, Cambridgeshire Virtual School)

The Pupil Premium Plus

The Pupil Premium Plus (PPP) is an extension of the Pupil Premium, which was first introduced by the Government in 2011 for children eligible for free school meals, children whose parents serve in the armed forces, and looked after children; its purpose was to close the attainment gap between these groups and their peers. In 2013, the Department for Education introduced the PPP exclusively for looked after and previously looked after children. In doing so, the Government acknowledged the lasting impact of trauma and loss in children's lives and the key role of schools in supporting children who have had a difficult start in life.

The PPP is a Government grant to schools to help them meet the needs of adopted children and currently brings £2,300 to a school per adopted child (2018–2019). Children who are educated at home or who attend private schools aren't eligible unless the placement is funded by the local authority.

This money is not ring-fenced for use with an individual child; the school can, if they wish, pool it for the benefit of a number of children.

Stuart Guest is the head teacher at Colebourne Primary School in Birmingham and is also an adoptive father. He writes a regular blog about schools, education and adoption, and says that he is often asked by parents about schools' use of the PPP. Here's an extract from his very informative blog post on this subject:

'Do parents have a say about how PPP is used?'

The simplest answer is No! But, there are a few things I would say you could do. The first thing is to build the relationship with the school to enable your voice to be listened to and not just heard.

The second thing would be to look for broad impact strategies that can be built on – for me this is whole school attachment training. If schools have not had this I would expect the PPP money to be used to at least train a few key people and preferably the whole school.

Also, be as specific as you can be with schools as to what you feel would help your child. Back it up with information from other professionals – especially if you have accessed the Adoption Support Fund. For example, you may want to improve your child's impulse control or specific aspects of executive functioning. Get the provision planned around this.

Finally, make the link to achievement if needed (especially for those schools that care more about academic achievement than social and emotional support). If you can show that once your child feels safe/is regulated then their learning outcomes will increase, the school may be more willing to support their emotional needs when they see this!

Remember, there remains a huge knowledge gap in many schools about attachment and developmental trauma and as such many schools are not aware of the best ways to support children who have these needs or the impact that certain traditional approaches can have on these children.

Remember, parents and schools can contact the Virtual Head for their area and ask for guidance on the effective use of the Pupil Premium Plus.

(Guest, 2018)

Sometimes, of course, the PPP can be used for individual support that might not otherwise have been available:

Two-and-a-half years in, and we have finally persuaded the school to allocate some of Cameron's Pupil Premium Plus to her individual needs and this is now funding some tuition (with her friend who is also adopted) for them both to have 2:1 tuition three mornings a week for 20 minutes with their class teacher... We feel strongly that if this had been applied when she first joined, then the gap between her and her peers would not be as wide as it is now.

(Karen Wilkins, adoptive mother)

Share your child's adoptive status with her school before the Christmas holidays (if you haven't already done so), to allow the school to claim the Pupil Premium Plus in the January schools census. Provide a photocopy of the adoption order (you can blank out certain details if you want). If your child changes school, you need to declare it again.

Be proactive about communicating with the school

Primary schools tend to be better at regular home–school communication than secondary schools.

The most important way you can work with your child's school is by sharing with them what you know about your child. You can give the school and teachers hugely important insights into what will work best for her.

However, this does take a lot of time and energy on your part. Also, you will probably have to do the same at the start of every school year, as teachers change.

- When your child joins a school, meet and get to know key support staff such as the designated teacher, SENCO or pastoral lead and work with them so that the school knows what the likely issues might be.

- Do this early on, before any problems arise.

- From the start, ask the teacher, designated teacher or SENCO if you can have regular meetings to discuss your child's progress (or the school may be able to set up an EPAC, as explained above). Regular meetings are a good idea even if things are going well, but of course the teacher may have other more pressing priorities if your child is doing fine. In this case, you might need to make it a shorter meeting or a check-in phone call instead for a while. When times get tough, it helps if you've already built a relationship and you can all reflect on things that the child has been able to do well before.

- Make a "profile" about your child, with her help. This can be a one-page sheet that describes what she likes, what she doesn't like, anything she might find particularly difficult and what might help, and so on. This can then be shared with all the teachers who are likely to come into contact with your child.

- Arrange for the school to give you advance notice of any changes coming up in school that might affect your child.

- It can be helpful for the school if you are able to tell them about anything coming up for the child at home that could potentially be upsetting – such as letterbox contact, face-to-face birth family contact – or if you have had to break bad news to the child.

- Your child might not know or might not want to tell you about homework or what's coming up at school but – at least in secondary school – children are usually given both a timetable and a home–school diary (a communication tool between parents and staff), so you can check.

  From my point of view it's important to be as open and honest as it's possible to be with the right people in school so they have a good understanding of the situation and you can support them in getting it right. Communication is key. If you sit back and don't say anything, they are not going to understand or be aware of the needs.

  (Claire Hiorns, personal communication)

Hiorns recommends that adoptive parents find out who is the designated teacher for post-looked after children and arrange to meet with that person and the class teacher.

Many adoptive parents who are new to all this wonder how often they can go into school without being considered pushy or overprotective. This is one of the things Cambridgeshire Virtual School has covered in its training for schools, says Hiorns, and teachers have been gaining more understanding of the situation of adoptive parents.

One thing we sometimes get from schools [about adoptive parents] is 'they are incredibly anxious and it's as though they think their child is the only one we've got', so one of the things we've been trying to help schools do is to place themselves in the shoes of an adoptive parent and understand where these anxieties are coming from. I think if the school get it right in terms of the relationship with the family and showing the parents that they have also got the child's best interests at heart and that they are listening, that is going to alleviate a lot of those anxieties. All the parents want to know is that their child is safe and that they are happy and making progress.

(Claire Hiorns, personal communication)

How much should you tell the school about your child's circumstances before you adopted them?

This is a very personal decision. Some information is obviously going to help your child's teachers to understand him or her better, but you will want to keep certain things back. Check with whom the information is going to be shared; it should be on a "need to know" basis.

I was at a meeting at a secondary [school] where parents wanted to share with the staff the extremes of what their child had been through. The teachers said 'Wow, OK, no wonder he was a bit difficult in my class. If he has lived with that, I'm more prepared to deal with it and more willing to – not overlook it, but acknowledge where those behaviours are coming from.' So it can be extremely powerful – it's just whether or not parents feel comfortable.

(Helen Hoban, Head of Education, PAC-UK, personal communication)

Should parents ask their child before sharing information with teachers?

Rather than asking the question, it might be better to have a conversation and say, 'We think it's really important that your teachers understand some things in order to make sure they can keep you feeling safe at school'. If parents say, 'Here are some things that we think they might need to know, how do you feel?' or 'Pick the two things you think are most important', the child still gets some say in it but also the parent is still steering it. Even at secondary school I'm not sure how able some children would be to make that decision.

(Helen Hoban, Head of Education, PAC-UK, personal communication)

Managing trauma triggers and curriculum hotspots

If you know what triggers traumatic memories for your child, make the school aware of these things.

For example, if your child really struggles with loud noises, you may need to say: 'Because of something that happened in early life, sudden loud noises are a real problem for Jane so here are some strategies to help her cope'. Or: 'How can you as a school minimise the impact of the fire alarm? Can she have some earplugs in her pocket to use, and can staff be made aware that she can wear them, so she is not told off for it?'

When you are letting your child's teacher know that he or she is adopted and what issues or behaviour might crop up, ask the teacher to discuss it with you if there is anything coming up in the curriculum that might be a difficult issue for your child.

There are many ways in which teachers can manage these situations in a supportive way, points out Claire Hiorns of Cambridgeshire Virtual School, who provides training for schools on how to support adopted children:

We talk about, where possible, adapting the content for the whole class so the whole class are still meeting the learning outcomes but they are not doing something different for the child, so the child doesn't feel singled out.

If they are doing a topic with bringing in baby pictures, they can say, 'Bring in a picture of when you were younger,' which could mean three weeks ago. As for looking at family trees, it doesn't have to be a personal family tree; they could look at the family tree of a famous person, or they could look at presenting it differently so it's not just a tree, it's an orchard, so they are considering the complexities.

All of that needs to be discussed with the family and thought about in terms of the implications. We also talk about what that might do to the behaviour, not just in that session but the wider context. The child might need a key adult with them. All the way through we talk about there's no "one size fits all", every child is different, every family is different, therefore, it's about having that communication and thinking about them as an individual and planning accordingly.

Groups for adoptive parents

Some schools have set up groups for adoptive parents, so that they can offer moral support to each other and also speak as one voice to the school about policies affecting their children, e.g. approaches to managing behaviour and the PPP. If your child's school doesn't have such a group, why not link up with other adoptive families yourself?

Supporting your child through transitions

Major transitions, such as the start of a new school year or moving to a new school, as well as minor transitions such as moving from classroom to classroom or from school to home at the end of the day, can be challenging for many adopted children. When a child has had times in her life when she has felt unsure or unsafe and lacked a sense of a "secure base", a transition can trigger the anxiety and fear she has felt before.

Some transitions are a big leap for children and parents alike. You might be worried about how your child is going to cope in a new class or new school. You need, of course, to be accepting of her feelings about the upcoming changes and acknowledge that she may be feeling worried or scared – but also try to anticipate the positives and be excited about the change when you talk with her about it, so that you transmit positive feelings rather than your anxiety.

Strategies that might help when your child starts school or makes the transition to secondary school are outlined in Chapters 4 and 7.

The following suggestions can help with other types of transition:

- Ask the school to give you prior warning, for example, if there is going to be a substitute teacher or change of classroom, so that you prepare your child by talking it through with them in advance.

- If there's going to be a school trip, your child could take a "transitional object" with her (see below). Ask staff if the itinerary can be adapted to meet her needs, e.g. perhaps she could join the class for the daytime activities only, rather than staying overnight, or join a residential trip half way through so she is not away for so long.

- You may be able to prepare your child for a trip or something like sports day by showing her photos or taking her to the actual place where she will be going.

- Ask the teacher if it's possible to provide your child with signs or a storyboard showing what the class will do and when – assembly, maths, reading, lunchtime, breaktime, etc.

- Have the school timetable or a visual representation of the school day in a prominent place at home, such as on the fridge, so your child can see what is going to happen day by day.

- A new school bag, new pencils, etc, may help your child to feel more positive about the change.

- If you can, get involved in the life of the school. For instance, if you help out on school trips and fundraising events, your child will see that you are working together with the school, and you will be able to be present at some events to help her feel more secure.

- PAC-UK has useful tip sheets on the education resources page on its website, entitled Goodbyes and Transitions, and Reducing Trip Trauma (www.pac-uk.org/education-resources/).

Separation anxiety

When a child is adopted, it can take some time to form attachments to new parents. Going to school for a full day can seem like a long time to be away from these recent attachment figures; she or he may wonder if their new parents will still be there at the end of the day or if they will forget them while they are out of sight. If necessary, it may be possible for your child to attend school part-time at first to mitigate these worries..

When a child has separation anxiety, giving them a "transitional object" to take to school can help. This is something they can keep with them to remind them of you, and to remind them that you are thinking of them during the day and will be there when school finishes. It could be any small item that evokes home, such as a small soft toy or a handkerchief with your scent on it.

If the teacher is another attachment figure for your child, it can also help for them to give the child something to take home (e.g. at weekends or holidays) to remind the child that the teacher is holding the child in mind; for example, some small item from the classroom for the child to "look after".

Having to peel a crying child away from you in order to make them go into school is a painful experience for both of you, especially when it goes on day after day. Ask the school what they suggest. Having a familiar member of staff or key person to greet your child in the playground when you arrive at school and perhaps take them into school before the rest of the children may make the parting a little easier.

Another way to alleviate separation anxiety is to volunteer within the school, even though you may well not be allowed to do so within your child's class:

The fact that you are on school premises some days means the child "holds you in mind" and feels you are part of their world when at school. Volunteering to read, help with the library or with the parent–teacher association are great opportunities not only to be around more at school but also to get to know the teaching and support staff. It helps with communication also.

(Karen Wilkins, adoptive mother)

When the school isn't getting it

Building trust and relationships and helping the child feel safe and accepted are the key to success at school as well as at home. But not all teachers and schools "get it", as this adoptive father explains:

They all love Tom and want to do their best for him but we've had to learn, as parents, how to parent this boy, which is something that most parents wouldn't recognise as parenting. But the school keeps saying to me: 'Are there any sanctions you use at home that work?' Well no, that's not how you deal with these children. I say, 'We don't have sanctions,' and they look at me aghast. They say, 'Well, what are the boundaries and discipline?' and I say, 'That's not how it works. It's all about relationships and building trust.' What matters is building the trust and we've done it, it's worked at home. I won't say it's easy – it's bloody difficult – but it's a different way of parenting and it has to be a different way of educating.

(Adoptive father, personal communication)

If you feel the school isn't listening to you sufficiently or you don't feel you are getting things across, sometimes it can help to have input from a professional who can speak to the staff and advocate on your child's behalf. Some parents ask their post-adoption social worker or someone from the virtual school, for example, to attend meetings with them.

If parents want the school to have a better understanding of their child's needs or when a child is not managing, the virtual school may be able to offer advice and guidance to the parents and the school. Citing Claire Hiorns again:

We would ask the parents to go back and speak to the school and say, we are available to support and would the school welcome contact?

It's got to be done in partnership with the school. So far all parties have been very open to the idea. If they are finding things difficult then they welcome advice and guidance.

As well as virtual schools, other organisations such as PAC-UK, local Special Educational Needs and Disability Information and Advice Services, post-adoption support and educational consultancies may be able to work in partnership with schools to address issues with individual children or the school as a whole (see Appendix/Further resources).

When others ask you and your child about adoption

You will want to discuss with your child how and what she shares with peers about her adoption story. This can, of course, be an issue for parents too, when other parents ask questions. You can talk to your child about why she may choose to keep her adoption and/or experiences "private" (but not "secret") and whom she can safely confide in at school.

Helen Hoban, Head of Education at PAC-UK, suggests a few strategies for helping you and/or your child tackle difficult questions:

> *It can be a big issue. In primary children can be unpleasant. Children can be very open and tell everybody and then it comes back in Year 6 and Year 7 and in secondary school it's used in bullying. We do a training day for parents and one of the things we advise is practising with your child when that question comes up and owning their story. It's twofold: What do you want people to know? They might say they are happy for everybody to know everything. Then as parents you can hone that down slightly and say, 'OK, great that you want to be open, why don't we choose three things that you can tell? Maybe don't tell everybody everything yet but these are the three things that you share.'*

> *And then you practise together over and over and they have got that to fall back on. The other thing is, what would you do if somebody came up and said, 'You're adopted, aren't you?' What are some general responses you could have?*

> *We use the acronym WISE up – walk away, ignore, share, educate more generally – quite often for the parents as much as for the child, if someone says 'What happened to your child?' or 'Adopted children have all been abused, haven't they, what's your kid's story?' Sadly adults do do this.*

> *You can turn it around and instead of answering their question you can say, 'Yes, unfortunately quite a lot of children do go through difficult experiences before they are adopted – anyway, see you later, bye.'*

> *"Walk away and ignore" go against what we normally teach our children. We say don't ignore people, don't walk away when someone is talking to you, but in certain circumstances if someone is being rude or asking about something you don't want to talk about it is OK to say, 'I don't want to talk about this, thank you' and walk away.*

> *We talk a lot about practising because a child can feel anxious about answering that question or feel caught on the spot. If they haven't had the chance to practise it at home in a comfortable environment with their parents then they might not feel able to access that information in the heat of the moment.*

Both children and adults are naturally curious but can sometimes ask intrusive questions that might leave you or your child feeling uncomfortable and awkward.

> *Let your child know who they can trust and approach in school if they have a burning question or need to discuss something in relation to their adoption that cannot wait until home time. Caution them against confiding in their peers. Friendships at primary school age can be volatile and inconsistent and information shared with a "friend" can sometimes be used against an adopted child. Children from the wider population are likely to have scant understanding of adoption – this is also true of many adults. Being singled out as the "adopted kid" is something adopted children are incredibly fearful of, as they generally want to fit in and be accepted. It is therefore critical to have a discussion with the child about who they can confide in within the school setting. We discussed this with the school's LAC (looked after children) lead and shared our daughter's background with her (including information around having direct contact with birth siblings, which can be a trigger for her). It means that my daughter knows she can go and see Mrs S at any time and she will feel safe and listened to.*

(Karen Wilkins, adoptive mother)

Homework

This sometimes causes real stress and conflict in adoptive families.

> *I think as parents we all want to do what the school bids us and what others seem happy/more than able to manage, but then feel inadequate when our children hit the homework wall.*

(Karen Wilkins, adoptive mother)

If your child struggles to do the homework, even with your help, it may not be worth making a big issue out of it and possibly damaging the relationship you are building with them. If homework is an issue in your house, talk to the teacher about what support is available or could be put in place, such as a homework club. If it continues to be a problem, perhaps explain why you are not willing to force your child to complete homework if it's going to cause them a lot of stress.

Stuart Guest, head teacher of Colebourne Primary School in Birmingham and an adoptive father, is not a big believer in the value of homework in primary school and says he told his children's school that they would not necessarily be doing their homework. 'We don't let homework in our house damage relationships – the school can deal with it,' he says. He does make "homework time" as nice as possible for the children, with hot chocolate and biscuits, but doesn't allow it to become a big issue if the children really do not want to do it.

- Have set days and times for homework.

- Make it as pleasant a time and place as you can.

- Show you are willing to help.

- Think of something positive for your child for when she has done it, such as playing a game together.

- If your child is refusing to do it, you might want to consider adopting Stuart Guest's approach – especially with older children. They will see the consequences of not doing homework coming from the school, rather than from you.

Adoptive mother Karen Wilkins says that while she sees homework as a good "habit" for children to form, it is also important to differentiate the home and school environment, and home should not feel like a classroom:

In our school there is a homework club on a Tuesday lunchtime which children are free to attend if they have not finished their homework task at home. They have support from teachers within this group and can choose whether to attend or not...We try to make homework time something to do at the start of the weekend, to get it out of the way. If it isn't completed within a 20-minute window, then we put the books away and go and do something fun.

Safeguarding for adopted children

As an adoptive parent, you may want to be sure your child will not feature in school photos or reports of school events on the school website or in the press. Check with the school about its photography/publicity policy and how this will impact on your child.

While the school will have a policy to ensure your child's photo is not featured on the website, etc., there are other softer issues that may crop up, such as the child appearing in a school play and other parents recording the performance and putting it on social media. Our school has a "no recording" policy during any performance, but balances the needs of other parents who wish to have a recording of a performance by re-running a song or two from the play at the end of the show. Children who are not, for whatever reason, wanting to be part of this are asked to return to the classroom. This needs to be handled sensitively in order to avoid singling out any individual children.

(Karen Wilkins, adoptive mother)

Obviously you will let the school know if you are concerned about the risk of your child's birth relatives attempting to find or contact your child. (If it's a pre-adoptive placement, schools should have received this information from social workers.) If necessary, a safeguarding plan should be put in place. This would include the child only being handed over to you as the carer or a named person and may involve the use of a password. If you are going to be late to collect your child, notify the school as soon as you can so that they can ensure that she is with an appropriate person who knows with whom she can go home.

Each school has a designated teacher responsible for child protection and safeguarding (often the head teacher) and this teacher should also be responsible for any privacy concerns.

Cherry Newby is a former primary head teacher and now adoptive mother. The following advice comes from her blog post on how parents can work with the school to safeguard their child:

As a head teacher, I had a number of adopted children in the school and often came up against these issues. As an adoptive parent, I have been on the other side of the fence, and have learnt how to approach schools to ensure that my child is as safe as possible when they are not with me. Here are my top tips.

Names

If your child has not yet been adopted then the school will have their birth surname on the records. This makes perfect sense for schools as officially the child's name hasn't been changed. However, from a parent's point of view, we don't want their birth name on all documents, books, etc. The easiest way around this is to speak to the school as early as you can and ask that the child 'be known as' your surname, and that this is written on all documents and books. This should quickly solve the problem and ensure that, when your child is adopted, the process to change their name formally is smooth and quick.

Websites/blogs

It is a Government requirement that all primary schools maintain an up-to-date website full of important statutory information. However, lots of schools take this further and have class blogs or put pictures and information about what is going on each week on their website. The concern here is how to keep your child's photo off the website or blog. This is a pretty easy fix. All schools should ask you to complete a data protection form which allows you to give, or refuse, permission for photos. Schools are generally good at checking these forms but it is always worth checking the website on occasions in case a photo slips through (this could be because it's a whole school photo or class photo), in which case a gentle reminder to the school office will rectify it immediately.

Newsletters

This was a surprise one to me as a parent, but when my daughter won a prize her name was put onto the newsletter as her full name. Admittedly it was her adopted surname but I was uncomfortable about having any child's full name on a newsletter, so I spoke with the school who agreed and amended their policy so only the first name, or first name and initial of their surname was published.

Use the key word!

Sometimes, just sometimes, you will run into something that the class teacher can't (or won't) sort out or understand. So at this point, your best plan of action is to ask for a meeting with the head teacher and, when questioned about why you need a meeting, mention the key words: "safeguarding issues". This will get you in to see the head and will solve the problems quickly. However, you should use this strategy only when you really need to, otherwise it can damage your relationship with the class teacher if they don't feel trusted.

Lock-down

My final piece of advice is something I call "lock down". I came up with this in my first year as a Head when a birth parent was known to be phoning schools in the local area to try to identify which school their child attended. We introduced a "lock down" policy. Essentially this meant that the adoptive parents gave the school a list of people who might call the school (sometimes including social workers) and whom we could talk to about their child. If anyone else called, the office staff were instructed to say that there was no child by that name at the school and to immediately phone the adoptive parent.

Schools can be difficult places to negotiate and sometimes I find myself thinking 'How did this happen?' or 'Didn't they think?' It's at times like this that I take a step back and remember that schools and teachers are just people too, and mistakes do happen – it's what happens after the mistake has been pointed out that is important, and educating the school or teacher on the issues that can arise so that these mistakes aren't repeated in the future.

(Newby, 2016)

Key points

- If you can, have regular meetings with key people at your child's school.

- The school might set up an educational support plan for your child so they can keep tabs on her well-being and progress.

- Make a "profile" of your child, with your child's help, so that all school staff will be aware of important things about her.

- Communicating with the school takes effort but it can help to ensure they understand your child's possible issues and triggers, make adjustments and ease him or her through transitions.

- If problems arise, having pre-existing good relationships can be invaluable.

6 Rights, special needs support, exclusion and alternative provision

Admissions

Local authorities are obliged to offer every child a school place. Many schools are oversubscribed, but looked after children and adopted children must be given the highest priority when it comes to admissions, even if the school is oversubscribed. This means your child should be able to attend whichever school you think best meets their needs, including local authority schools, academies and free schools. (Selective schools are an exception, however. They are allowed to prioritise on the grounds of ability and the standards against which they are selected should be published. If they don't fill all their places on the grounds of those criteria, the rest of the admissions code applies as usual.)

If you are having problems finding a school place, contact the person in the local authority responsible for school admissions (their contact details can be found on the local authority website) and/or the virtual school head teacher.

Your local authority will have a web page and booklet for advice and guidance on how to apply for a school place in your area and how to contact those responsible for the admission process (see www.gov.uk/schools-admissions/admissions-criteria). There is a legal requirement that the school website shows how the Pupil Premium and Pupil Premium Plus money is spent and what it achieves, both of which are reviewed by Ofsted.

Ofsted grade educational settings as either: 'inadequate', 'requiring improvement', 'good' or 'outstanding'.

To find a recent report for a school, look at the Ofsted website: http://reports.ofsted.gov.uk/.

Special educational needs

If a child is adopted when very young, it is rarely easy to predict what needs or difficulties might emerge as he grows. Special educational needs (SEN) and disabilities – e.g. learning difficulty, attachment disorder, FASD, autism – are not always obvious at the time of the adoption but may become apparent later on when he starts school or sometimes only when it becomes clear the child cannot cope with the increased complexity of functioning in a secondary school.

Disabled children

Schools have to make "reasonable adjustments" for disabled children. These can include:

- changes to physical features, e.g. adding a ramp;
- changes to how learners are assessed;
- providing extra support and aids, e.g. specialist teachers or equipment.

A useful resource is the Council for Disabled Children website (https:// councilfordisabledchildren.org.uk). Select "Help & resources" and the option "I'm a parent", which takes you to all content aimed at parents.

Education, Health and Care Plans

An Education, Health and Care Plan (EHCP) is for children and young people aged up to 25 who need more support than the usual provision of special educational needs support in school.

An EHCP identifies the child's educational, health and social needs and sets out the additional support that should be provided to meet those needs.

Requesting an EHC assessment

A request to the local authority for an assessment, can be made by teachers, parents and other people, including doctors. A young person is entitled to request an assessment themselves if they're aged 16 to 25.

If the local authority decides to carry out an assessment, you may be asked for:

- any reports from your child's school, nursery or childminder;
- medical assessments of your child;
- a letter from you about your child's needs.

The local authority will tell you within 16 weeks whether an EHCP is going to be made for your child.

Independent support for children of all ages

Independent supporters can help you and your child through the SEN assessment process. Ask your SENCO about this or contact your local Special Educational Needs and Disability Information and Advice Service (SENDIAS).

Creating an EHCP

1. Your local authority will create a draft EHCP and send you a copy.

2. You have 15 days to comment, including if you want to ask that your child goes to a special needs school or specialist college.

3. Your local authority has 20 weeks from the date of the assessment to give you the final EHCP.

If your child meets the EHCP threshold, the local authority will recommend a school for them. If you apply there, the school must give your child a place.

If your child does not meet the EHCP threshold (which is quite high), he or she will continue to be given special educational needs support in school.

Disagreeing with a decision

You can challenge your local authority about:

- their decision to not carry out an assessment;
- their decision to not create an EHCP;
- the special educational support in the plan;
- the school named in it.

If you can't resolve the problem with your local authority, you can appeal to the Special Educational Needs and Disability (SEND) Tribunal (see https://www.gov.uk/courts-tribunals/first-tier-tribunal-special-educational-needs-and-disability).

Personal budgets

Depending on the level of your child's disability, you may be able to get a personal budget for your child if they have an EHCP or have been told that they need one.

Also make sure you are claiming all the benefits and help you are entitled to if you are the parent of a child with a disability (see https://www.gov.uk/help-for-disabled-child).

EHCP system failings

On the ground, the EHCP process does not always work as well as it should. Many parents feel that it is a battle to get this plan for their child and a very isolating experience.

Families of children with special educational needs sometimes face a "disproportionate burden" to ensure that they get the support they need, according to a report issued by the Local Government and Social Care Ombudsman in October 2017.

The report looks at the common issues seen by the Ombudsman in its first 100 investigations into complaints about EHCPs after their introduction in 2014 to replace SENs.

The new system was designed as a more holistic way of providing SEN support for children. It is supposed to make it easier. But in reality, for some families it is not.

Michael King, Local Government and Social Care Ombudsman, said:

'When councils get things wrong it places a disproportionate burden on families already struggling with caring and support: some families have to go well beyond the call of duty to confirm the type of support their children should receive.

'We issued a report in March 2014, highlighting the shortcomings which needed to be addressed with the new EHCP system. Regrettably, our first 100 investigations show this has not happened.

'The system is not failing universally. But for those people who come to us, we are finding significant problems – sometimes suffering long delays in getting the right support and children ultimately failing to reach their potential.'

(Local Government and Social Care Ombudsman, 2017)

Many plans are not being completed on time.

The Ombudsman's report highlights some of the common issues investigators have found in their first 100 cases. One of the overriding features is significant delay in the process. Others issues include: failing to involve parents and young people properly in the decision-making process; not gathering sufficient evidence to inform decisions; and a lack of proper forward planning when young people move between key educational stages.

(More information and help on SEND is available at www.gov.uk/children-with-special-educational-needs/special-educational-needs-support.)

A key resource is the legal handbook available at https://councilfordisabled children.org.uk/help-resources/resources/disabled-children-legal-handbook-2nd-edition. Contact your local SENDIAS service by going to https://councilfordisabledchildren.org.uk/information-advice-and-support-services-network/find-your-local-ias-service.

You can also:

- Search for the "local offer" on your local authority's website.

- Consult your local authority's VSH.

- Contact IPSEA (Independent Parental Special Education Advice, www.ipsea.org.uk).

- Contact the Council for Disabled Children (as above).

There are many support groups, both online and in person and Facebook groups of parents who are going through similar things – linking up with other parents is often really supportive. For example, the FASD UK Facebook Support Group is a closed Facebook group and an online support community for people with FASD and those who care for them: see www.facebook.com/groups/FASDUK/.

Applying for an EHCP – one adoptive father's story

We spoke to an adoptive father about the process of applying for an EHCP for his son Tom. This is what he told us:

We adopted Tom when he was three and he is now seven.

He is a charismatic, funny, active, sporty fellow. But when he started school at nearly five, it quickly became apparent that the more traditional learning aspects of the school curriculum were very hard for him. He is now in Year 3, and he is basically unable to access the curriculum – his ability to concentrate is practically zero because his emotional needs are so marked and he is finding the boundaries and discipline of school extremely threatening.

The school are trying very hard but we've had a patchy record of appropriate support for him. At one point in Year 2 they did give him a one-to-one teaching assistant who was excellent. She seemed to understand that this was all about relationships and giving him emotional security, which enabled him to relax enough to start doing some learning and he was making good progress. But then she was moved on abruptly. He'd been told that she was going to be staying but then she was moved with no warning at all. That was a very bad failing on the part of the school that broke his trust with the school. We've never really got him back to a good place after that.

He is in a constantly heightened state. He perceives everybody as shouting at him although they are not. They put in some better support this term, in that there is someone he can go to if he is feeling dysregulated in class and kicking off in class but it's not a sustainable level of support because she's a deputy head and can't give him her full time attention.

We have had to push, push and push to get the EHCP. The school was very reluctant to engage with this process. It's because it's a lot of hard work and they don't have the resources for people to do it. I have been pushing the SENCO for the best part of a year to get the EHCP process going and she kept saying, 'Yes, we are doing what we need to do', and nothing had been done.

It's taken an inordinately long time and I've sensed resistance to it from the SENCO, from the head teacher, from all around. The EHCP means that the school has to sign up to a level of provision that they are under a statutory obligation to provide once the plan is in place. I was quite surprised at how resistant the school was to getting the plan because I thought the plan means they will get some financial support and support from other agencies to help our son at school, because they can't do it on their own.

We did get the school to apply for the EHCP but I had to tell them that I was going to do it myself if they didn't. They are not used to parents being very proactive on these things. So I said to them in the end, 'We are going to apply for this now if you don't get the paperwork off by such and such a deadline'. And I got the local SENDIAS (special educational needs and disability information and advice service) on side and we had a "team around the child" meeting – parents, teachers, social worker, CAMHS and the educational psychologist – and then the ball started rolling properly.

We've got the EHCP but it's not been finished yet. The local authority presents a draft of the plan and we have what's called a co-production meeting, a day for all interested parties, teachers, parents, CAMHS team – we all get together and discuss what's in it and what isn't in it. It's a chance for us to have our say so, as you can imagine, I'm going in with a list of points as long as your arm.

I am hoping for one-to-one support. It's essential. If he doesn't get it I will remove him from the school.

I don't feel confident that he is emotionally safe at the school. He's fallen so far behind. We are considering as a very last resort moving him to a school that can deal with him but that would be an absolute last resort because he would hate being moved. For all the problems that he has there, he has a very strong connection to that school and he's got a lot of friendships there. He finds them quite hard to manage but they are very important people to him so we are extremely reluctant to move him.

Some days later, Tom's father gave us this update:

We had the EHCP co-production meeting a couple of weeks ago, and the plan is now being finalised. However, it's become abundantly clear that the current school is unable to meet his needs, things are getting worse by the day and we had an exclusion last week. I'm now in the process of finding a better school for him.

Exclusion

Here are the facts about exclusion.

The head teacher and teachers at a child's school may feel the behaviour or problems a child is presenting are unacceptable. They may, therefore, decide to exclude the child. This is normally for grossly challenging behaviour or a serious specific incident.

But the Government's statutory guidance makes it clear that the school should involve the designated teacher if an adopted child is at risk of exclusion, and he or she should talk to you and seek the advice of the virtual school head on how to avoid excluding your child:

> When a child leaves care, their past experiences may continue to impact on their behaviour. As with looked after children, the school should look to support the child to improve their behaviour to avoid exclusion becoming necessary. Where a previously looked after child is at risk of exclusion, the designated teacher should talk to the child's parents or guardians before seeking the advice of the VSH on avoiding exclusion.

> (Department for Education, March 2018, p. 32)

There are two kinds of exclusion: fixed-term and permanent.

Fixed-term exclusion (suspension)

This is an exclusion for a set period of time, normally less than five days. It must not exceed 45 days in a single year. Only the head teacher can authorise an exclusion. For any exclusion over five days, the head teacher must make alternative arrangements and notify the parent/carer of these arrangements.

The responsibility for the child while they are on a fixed-term exclusion is that of the parent or carer. They are legally required to ensure that the child is not present in public places during school hours. This may mean that you will need to supervise their activity during the time of their exclusion.

Permanent exclusion

Permanent exclusion occurs when a child will no longer be able to continue to attend the school. Your local authority will support finding your child alternative school or education provision. This type of exclusion should only happen if other methods have been tried and are not working or a child has been involved in a serious first time offence, such as violence or drug abuse.

Alternatives to exclusion

There are alternatives to fixed-term and permanent exclusions. They could include removal of a child from class to a unit within school, a strategy used with many children presenting challenging behaviour or with behavioural, emotional or social difficulties. There may be an internal exclusion in which a child works in isolation away from their class, but is supervised by a member of staff. Lunchtime exclusions may occur if the challenging behaviour or incidents form a pattern at break times. Also, consideration of a temporary part-time timetable may be suitable if a child is struggling with integration (Alix and Fisher, 2018).

Unofficial exclusions

There is some concern that the Government's figures for official school exclusions represent just the tip of the iceberg, and that there are many more cases of illegal "unofficial" exclusions and "off-rolling", where children are leaving school rolls in "managed moves" between schools or transferred to off-site alternative provision (some of which will be independent and unregistered) while others disappear into allegedly "elective" home education.

Adoption UK carried out a survey of adoptive parents in 2017, asking about their experiences of their children being excluded from school on a temporary or permanent basis. The charity is calling on the Government to collect and analyse exclusion and performance statistics for adopted children, as they do for other cohorts.

'Adopted children 20 times more likely to be excluded'

A survey of adoptive parents has found that their children were around 20 times more likely to be permanently excluded from school than their classmates... The survey, which received more than 2,000 responses from adoptive parents, also revealed that nearly a quarter (23 per cent) of their children had been temporarily excluded during their time at school.

The children of the adoptive parents who completed the survey were also 16 times more likely to be temporarily excluded during the first three years of primary school when compared with other children.

Official DfE statistics show that looked after children and SEND children are more likely to receive exclusions than their classmates. Adopted children share many of the same issues as looked-after children and are overly represented within the SEND cohort. But despite this, official figures for adopted children being excluded are not currently collected and analysed by the DfE.

Adoption UK's self-selecting survey is indicative, rather than scientific, yet raises serious concerns that adopted children are more likely to be excluded than their classmates.

Becky White, Adoption UK's schools development officer and the author of a report into the survey results, said:

> *'The comparatively high number of exclusions of very young adopted children is particularly disturbing. Many of these children will have only recently moved to their new adoptive families and are then experiencing significant disruptions to their education at a vulnerable point in their lives.*
>
> *Adoptive parents are the experts on their children. They're fully aware of the problems their children regularly face in school – but this survey reveals the shocking extent of these problems.'*

During the school year 2015–16, 15 per cent of adopted children represented in the survey had been informally excluded from school on a temporary basis – meaning their "exclusion" is not officially recorded. Of these children, almost a third had been informally excluded five or more times that year.

More than half (55 per cent) of adopted children who were excluded received no learning support at all during the exclusion period.

Ms White continued:

> *'The true extent of this problem is being masked because schools are regularly asking adoptive parents to take their children home and keep them out of school, without recording them as exclusions. More children were informally excluded in this way in 2015/16 than were formally excluded. We need to find better ways of improving the situation for children and teachers rather than relying on exclusions.*

The challenge for us now is in convincing education professionals that extra support is needed for adopted children from the start – instead of waiting until they are at crisis-point.

More than one in ten (12 per cent) of respondents said that their child's school advised them that the only way to avoid permanent exclusion was for them to voluntarily remove their child – generally referred to as a "managed move".'

(Adoption UK, 2017)

Alternative provision

Alternative provision includes things like Pupil Referral Units (either attached to a school or stand-alone) and home tutoring for children who are not attending school.

The alternative provision offered to children who are excluded is often far from ideal. Here, an adopted 12-year-old describes their situation:

I'm 12 years old, nearly 13 and I'm adopted. I am writing this blog because I don't go to school because I went to a mainstream secondary school but I got beat up once and I got into a lot of trouble. I have HDHD [sic] and autism and something called FASD witch is when your mum drinks when you are in her belly and when you are born it effects your brain and the way you think. At the minute i am half way through getting assessed for a EHCP so i am sitting at home every day with a home tutor for an hour each day and then bored not knowing what to do. Me and my mum have looked round more than three special schools and we just have to wait.

Government to look into exclusion and alternative provision

In March 2018, the Government announced that it would look at the experience and outcomes for children who face the most challenges in mainstream school – including those at greatest risk of exclusion – such as those with SEN or autism, or children in need of help and protection, including those in care.

There will be a review of school exclusions, with a report due to be published at the end of 2018. It will look at a number of issues around exclusion, including:

- practice in schools in relation to behaviour management, identifying effective approaches that improve outcomes, particularly for those groups disproportionately likely to be excluded;

- practice in schools in relation to directing pupils to alternative provision without excluding;

- the drivers behind the variation in exclusion rates between schools with a similar intake.

(Department for Education, March 2018)

There will also be a £4 million fund to develop new ways to help children with additional needs move from alternative provision into mainstream or special schools, and measures to drive up standards in alternative provision settings.

If you want to challenge your child's exclusion

Meanwhile, you should contact the virtual school head for advice if you are told your child is to be excluded.

You'll get a letter from the school telling you what to do if you disagree with the exclusion.

You can ask the school's governing body to overturn the exclusion if either:

- your child has been excluded for more than five days; or

- the exclusion means they'll miss a public exam or national curriculum test.

If the exclusion is for five days or fewer, you can still ask the governors to hear your views but they can't overturn the head teacher's decision.

Challenging permanent exclusion

You'll be invited to a review meeting with the school's governors if your child has been permanently excluded. This will happen within 15 school days.

If the governors don't overturn the exclusion, you can ask for an independent review by your local council (or academy trust if the school's an academy). The governors must tell you how to do this.

If your child is still excluded you can ask the Local Government Ombudsman (or the Education Funding Agency if the school's an academy or free school) to look at whether your case was handled properly. They can't overturn the exclusion.

Moving your child to a new school: personal accounts

When school is not working out for your child, it can be a frustrating and upsetting experience for you all. If things have gone wrong, finding a school that will accept your child's difficulties and work with them can come as a huge relief.

The following blog was written by an adoptive parent whose attempts to work with her child's school were unsuccessful, but who found that her son thrived in his next school.

'Unattached to school'

Our son has been kicked out of school.

That is two-and-a-half years of almost constant struggle (and endless meetings) with the school reduced to just one line.

Two-and-a-half years of trying to get them to realise that his behaviour is not naughtiness and that it is controllable, two-and-a-half years of trying to make them understand his needs (which are quite typical of adopted and traumatised children) and the correct way to address them, two-and-a-half years of him suffering and consequently failing to get an education because of their inability to make him feel safe and calm.

Sadly, ultimately it boiled down to that one simple line and that is all that now matters for us.

The school tried – at times they tried very hard indeed – but their attempts were often misguided and sadly short lived. They would feel that they resolved one issue and another would raise its head and then they would simply give up. It has never felt that they were wanting to learn and to grow as a school, frustratingly it always felt like they were doing what was required to placate us – the frustrated, demanding parents. Without the belief that it was benefitting them too, I fear that their investment into it lacked any true conviction.

We never felt we had the understanding or the assistance of the SENCO to fight our corner, or from the "pastoral support teacher" who barely seemed to even understand pastoral care – so it always felt like a battle we were fighting alone and in hindsight we can see that it was one we were never destined to win.

The suggestion of finding him a "special school" was made regularly throughout the two-and-a-half years, yet nobody could tell us what kind of school he needed to be in or indeed where to find one.

Fortunately, we had started looking into alternatives and had found a school that seemed to offer an amazingly therapeutic approach within reasonable distance of where we live and which does indeed put the special needs of its children first and foremost.

However, we were yet to introduce ourselves to the school or indeed apply for admission for our son when on the last day of term the old school informed us that our son was no longer welcome there.

Thankfully the school we had found has been incredibly understanding and has accepted him pretty much immediately as they could see that it was a critical situation.

It's very early days and we are fully aware that we are in a "honeymoon period"; however, we are full of hope as so far things have been amazing. Our son is clearly at ease and comfortable in an environment that is welcoming and inclusive of his emotional needs.

They have not witnessed one issue so far and have said that his behaviour has been exemplary, and for the first time in a long while he is concentrating on work and he is actually achieving.

It is a total turnaround.

He is the same child, we are the same parents parenting in the same way that we always have – yet the old school just couldn't accept that THEY were failing him and creating the environment that was so difficult for him to function in.

Our son is not a bad child; in fact, family and friends around us are shocked when we share the issues that the school have been facing as they know a child who is nothing like the one the school knows.

Even if it is just a "honeymoon period" which comes to an end and the new school is subjected to the behaviour that the previous school struggled so deeply with, we know that they will still not see him as a bad boy and, just like we have learnt to do at home, they will see that they are doing something wrong and they will address the situation accordingly.

Isn't that what ALL schools should be doing?

(Reproduced with permission of We Are Family (2017), https://wearefamilyadoption. wordpress.com/2017/10/27/unattached-to-school/)

Moving your child to a different school can be a worrying time as you wonder if you have made the right choice. How will they cope with the transition? Will they thrive? But a move to a new school can be transformative, as this mother found when her son, who has FASD, moved to a specialist school.

The following blog is reproduced with permission from the adoptive parent who wrote it.

'The same child shines when seen through a different prism'

Our guy seems to learn in leaps. It's never a steady upward curve for him. He plateaus and then without any seeming rhyme or reason to it, he jumps up to the next level. Each time this happens, he falls back in other areas. Perhaps foolishly, each time it happens, we allow ourselves to be hit hard by the regression.

We are in one of those times. Our home environment is suffering. Our preteen son is increasingly armed with new vocabulary and new attitude, fuelled by a new edginess in what he is watching on YouTube. Social pressures at school are causing him great distress. He is getting less physical activity now that he is at a new school. His walks to and from school and his after-school activities have been replaced with time spent in a taxi. He is out of the house and "on" from 8:00 am until 4:00 pm. It's a long day for him.

When I snuck away to write this blog, I was feeling down. I was thinking of the rough morning we just had (diverted eventually by a walk along a river). I was still smarting from the rough night we had last night (diverted only by nearly two hours in a pool) and the string of other rough nights and rough mornings we have had lately. The mess of the house. Work stresses. The fact that this morning we rushed out of the house after a meltdown, in survival mode, and I haven't had a shower. Again. Yes, when I started writing I wasn't in a great mood.

Then I remembered that a school report arrived yesterday. I stepped away from the computer to have a read. Page by page, my mood lightened. Yes! It hit me. Our son may be regressing at home, but at school he is progressing in leaps and bounds. Once again, I am amazed at the difference it is making now that he is in a specialist setting.

Last year we were so crushed by our son's report card, we never let him see it. In contrast, this time I told him I had his school report and wanted to show him. He groaned and visibly moved away from me, alarmed and ready to bolt. I put my hand on his back and said, 'No, wait – it's excellent. Listen.' And we skimmed his in-depth report together. He became more and more excited. After one especially positive comment, he whispered with utmost pride, 'Maybe I should get a new toy!' (proving that at least in some cases he can link some cause and some effect and also showing, perhaps not flatteringly, that as parents we have not been above pure bribery in the past).

In a school that understands not all kids' brains are wired the same, here's what these new teachers wrote:

- *'He's an eager and enthusiastic pupil'*
- *'He has great ideas'*
- *'He is not at all afraid of thinking outside of the box'*
- *'His work benefits from his imagination'*
- *'He makes his presence felt with his enthusiasm'*
- *'He is keen to achieve good results'*
- *'He is gaining greater confidence'*
- *'He is a talented musician'*
- *'He has an ability to create exciting and engaging musical performances'*
- *'Polite'*
- *'Very able'*
- *'His attitude toward learning has been excellent'*
- *'His confidence has improved'*

- 'He has managed to express his colourful personality'

- 'I am delighted to have a pupil of such creativity and imagination at the school'

This is the same child who last year was chided in his report for "disruptive behaviour", for being "silly" and "distracting". The discouraged boy who was told he "needed to understand" his behaviour was "inappropriate". Who was marked down because he couldn't pay attention for "more than five minutes". The kid who we couldn't get out of the door to school because he was under so much pressure – this was happening as recently as five months ago.

I was especially struck by the comment on his current report from a science teacher. Last year, his science teacher commented on his final report that he repeatedly cried throughout the year when given instructions. Her reports were never positive, she saw only a problem student. Cue to this year, and here we are:

'He has worked hard in science lessons. He generally grasps new concepts quite quickly and enjoys the opportunities to work practically. He observes scientific experiences [experiments] carefully. He follows instructions well and can work in a careful, systematic manner.'

This is the same child.

He was so proud of this new report. We also talked about some of the comments that show his FASD is still affecting his ability to access education fully. He is starting to know these are areas where he always will have difficulty due to his FASD, areas where he will need to put strategies in place. When he read the bit about how he 'can easily become distracted and lose focus', he said: 'That happens sometimes, doesn't it?'

We acknowledged but brushed over the comments that 'he has yet to grasp cause and effect' and 'he must ensure he always listens carefully to an instruction so he knows what is expected of him'. We will continue to work with him to understand his FASD and also with his school to ensure they understand these challenges are not due to willful disobedience, but because he will always, for life, need instructions broken down – preferably shown in a visual format, maybe even rehearsed. Whereas previously these sorts of comments dominated his reports, this time, these comments were decidedly in the minority.

The most touching moment was when he asked me to explain this comment, the one that made my mood brighten most: 'He needs to believe in himself because he already has gained the respect of many of his peers.' We went over that together, slowly. As its meaning sunk in, he glowed.

It doesn't mean what's happening at home is not real, not concerning. Of course, when things are flying and getting broken we must hear what those behaviours are saying and make necessary changes. A positive report doesn't make his social challenges any less difficult. Recently he told me, heartbreakingly, that he is being bullied every day. But seeing this report does help me believe that those educators around him can help him get past that hurdle too. He may be having trouble with one or two kids, but he also is "earning the respect of many". Can you imagine how wonderful that is for a kid who has been sidelined by too many of his peers throughout too much of his education up to this point? We are on a whole new level. The setbacks at home have been accompanied by great progress in other areas.

Remembering that makes it all a bit easier.

(SB-FASD, blogpost, 2017)

Home schooling

Some parents decide the best option for their children is to educate them at home, at least for a while. Sadly, some feel that they are left with no choice but to do this because school is not working for their child and they have run out of options.

You can teach your child at home, either full- or part-time. You can home educate from the start if you like, but if you are taking your child out of school to home educate, you have to write to the head teacher to de-register your child. He or she will notify the local authority.

The head teacher must accept if you're taking your child out completely. However, they can refuse if you want to send your child to school some of the time (known as flex-schooling).

Local authorities get involved with home-educating families and offer support to varying degrees. The council can make an "informal enquiry" to check your child is getting a suitable education at home. They can serve a school attendance order if they think your child needs to be taught at school.

As a parent, you must make sure your child receives a full-time education from the age of five, but you don't have to follow the national curriculum.

Your council may be able to help if your child has special educational needs and you want to educate them at home. You need to tell them only if your child has an EHCP.

You can link up with other local families in the same situation and perhaps share skills to teach your children (try http://educationalfreedom.org.uk/find-a-local-group/ and https://educationotherwise.org/index.php/local-he-groups-directory) or get involved in online communities of home-educating parents. There is, of course, an infinite amount of educational resources on the internet.

Some useful resources:
www.educationotherwise.net
www.schoolhouse.org.uk (Scotland)
http://www.bbc.co.uk/education/highlights for learning resources

Key points

- When it comes to admissions, looked after and adopted children have to be given the highest priority, even when a school is oversubscribed.

- Education, Health and Care Plans (EHCPs) are available for children and young people up to 25 who need additional support beyond SEN.

- The exclusion of adopted children is all too common, even at a very young age, highlighting the need for more specialist support.

- Children who struggle in one school can flourish in a different school or type of school.

7 Starting at secondary school

Choosing a secondary school

Many of the questions you may need to ask overlap with those recommended for choosing a primary school (see Chapter 4). That said, several additional points relating to secondary education need to be considered when you are visiting schools to make your decision. Here are some more key questions compiled by PAC.

Key questions for secondary schools

How does the school provide consistent key relationships for children with attachment needs?

For example:

- *vertical form tutors (when a mixed aged group is taught together);*
- *nurture time/group;*
- *non-teaching pastoral staff available throughout the day;*
- *learning mentors;*
- *for children who receive one-to-one support, is support organised by child (i.e. one consistent teaching assistant) or by subject (i.e. up to 10 teaching assistants)?*

Where is the safe base for children when they need to calm down or regulate?

- *How does this work? Drop-in basis?*
- *Does the child need specific permission to attend?*
- *How is it staffed?*

- *Are any drop-in spaces staffed consistently?*

What is the behaviour management policy?

- *Does the school recognise that cause-and-effect consequences may not be effective for children with histories of trauma and loss?*

- *Does the school apply the policy flexibly to best meet the needs of each child?*

- *How does the school moderate its use of detention or Isolation for children who may be re-traumatised by these approaches?*

What support is in place for children who find unstructured times difficult?

For example:

- *lunch club;*

- *drop-in base;*

- *structured games in the playground;*

- *social skills groups.*

How does the school provide structure and consistency?

For example:

- *Year 7 in permanent base;*

- *lockers for children's belongings;*

- *vertical form tutor;*

- *approach to staff sickness and supply teachers;*

- *advance warning of timetable changes;*

- *building work, etc;*

- *timetable on the website so parents can prepare their child at home.*

How does the school support the Year 6 to Year 7 transition?

For example:

- *extra visits for vulnerable children;*
- *opportunities to see the school both empty and busy;*
- *maps and photos;*
- *summer club to get used to the school and key staff?*

How does the school share information with parents?

For example:

- *what equipment/kit is needed;*
- *homework timetable;*
- *web-based supported learning environment. Is this used by all staff? Do parents have log-ins?*

How does the school support children who find it difficult to manage their feelings?

For example:

- *nurture group;*
- *calm boxes;*
- *a calming zone within the school;*
- *emotion regulation skills teaching and coaching;*
- *anger management training;*
- *empathy from all staff.*

How does the school manage curriculum hotspots, i.e. issues that might trigger your child?

For example:

- *liaise with parents about sex, alcohol, drugs education;*

- *pass on information about any particular triggers to members of teaching staff.*

(Reproduced here with permission from PAC-UK)

Transition to secondary school

An 11-year-old starting secondary school will meet and have to interact with many more children, some of whom are likely to be familiar and friendly, but there will be many others who are unfamiliar and who appear scary, unpredictable, baffling or rejecting. Some adopted children will still be developing the skills they need to get on with other children. With new classmates come new pressures: making friends (which ones can be trusted?), keeping up with the rest of the class in lessons, holding your own, getting the jokes, looking right, wearing the right clothes, and keeping it together when you are feeling stressed. Instead of being the oldest year group in their primary school, they are suddenly the youngest – with many physically bigger, brasher, young people in the years above them in school – which can be daunting.

Children have to get to know lots of new teachers – ones who don't understand them yet – and they have several different teachers in the course of a day. There are new subjects and previously familiar subjects are taught in different ways. There's a bigger school to find your way around, more classrooms to navigate, more noise and crowds to contend with in the school corridors, new subjects to get to grips with, more things to organise to take with you in the morning, different school rules to understand and remember, and more homework to do. There's a new route to school, which may be longer than before, and possibly the hurdle of travelling independently to school for the first time, or using public transport when this has not previously been necessary.

All of these things are potential triggers for many adopted children. They are likely to be completely out of their comfort zone for quite some time.

Helping your child make the transition

Some of the things schools can do are listed above, in 'Key questions for secondary schools'. As a parent, you could also consider the following:

- Ask your child how she feels about going to secondary school and talk through any of the issues that are worrying her. If she tends to be uncommunicative, try going for a walk or a long drive somewhere together – that can help some children to open up.

- Take her to visit the school at busy times and quiet times. Photos and/or a map of the school might help some children understand the new layout.

- Take any opportunity to go to the Christmas fair, summer fair or any other events the school or parent–teacher association puts on that are open to the public.

- If your child is anxious about travelling to school by public transport, have several practice runs. Agree that you will do the home–school journey together a couple of times, then again with you following a short distance behind, then when she is confident let her do it by herself (or with a friend who will also be going to that school).

- Cultivate your child's friendships with children who will be going to the same secondary school (and do the same with their parents!).

- Do role-plays with your child of any situations that you think she might find difficult, such as introducing themselves to a new person or asking another child their name.

- Talk to your child about why she might want to keep her adoption story private, and role-play how she might respond if it comes up.

- Ask your child what she would like the teachers to know about her. If appropriate, involve her in putting together a profile that you can give to the school, or use what she has said when you are providing input into the Education Plan, if the school will be completing one of these for her.

- Be positive and enthusiastic about the new opportunities that the secondary school will offer – the range of sports, school facilities, the extracurricular clubs, bands, trips and other exciting things it has that primary school didn't.

- Help your child decide how she is going to say thank you and goodbye to her favourite people from her old school and help her to, for example, make cards and buy presents. Remind her that she can visit the school sometimes even after she has left.

- Remind her of ways in which she can keep in touch with some of her friends from her primary school if she will not be going to the same secondary school – such as going to Scouts or Brownies/Guides or going swimming together or to the cinema at weekends.

- Plan a treat for the first weekend after she starts at the new school, so she has something nice to look forward to once she has got through that first week.

- Remind your child of other times when she has been a bit nervous about going somewhere or doing something and has ended up really enjoying it.

What can help?

Many of the strategies to help adopted children discussed earlier in this book that help adopted children might seem more suited to primary schools than secondaries, but in fact they can be just as helpful for young people as for children.

A group of adopted young people were asked to look back on their school days and think about what could have made, or what did make, a difference. This is what they said:

- *a separate room for exams and a separate room in school with a key adult you can go to;*

- *time to talk to the teachers when you need to, or when you need to calm down if you are upset;*

- *'In secondary it was random teachers, like the chemistry teacher – a group of us could go and help him in break time to get away from the friendship dramas.'*

- *extra help and extra time in exams;*

- *'Drama helped me cope with everything I've been through.'*

There are nurturing secondary schools out there but it's harder to get right by the very nature of secondary schools, says Helen Hoban from PAC-UK. The organisation's advisers often work with secondary schools:

> *You need to find the developmental age of the child you are working with and apply strategies that are appropriate for that child.*

For example, when you would like a key person to meet with the child, it might be that you have to find a way to make that work in a secondary school where it's so much bigger and children say, 'I don't want to come and see you every morning, it's not cool.'

How do you make it work in a way that supports the child and feels achievable for the school? If the school thinks it's utterly impossible, they aren't going to implement anything. You could start with the idea that if each transition were to feel a little bit more supported for this child, how could we do that? Often schools will then lead the conversation and say, 'Well, Miss Appleby [the key person] could just be in the corridor, just be around casually so the child knows she's close by'. We say, 'Oh yes, that could work, could you facilitate that?' And if this is realistic schools will say, 'Absolutely, we can make that work.' The idea is to support schools in recognising the wealth of knowledge and resources they already have and help with ways to use those resources. Ultimately we all want the same thing, for the child to feel safe in school.

Whereas if you go in and say, 'He needs to have a teaching assistant for every single transition and they must walk into the lesson with him,' that can sometimes feel a bit much. Ideally we want schools to identify strategies that feel achievable leading from the questions and suggestions you make – then it is often better implemented and has more longevity and impact.

(Helen Hoban, Head of Education Service, PAC-UK, personal communication)

In secondary schools, young people are particularly aware of how they are viewed by their peers; they are keen to "blend in" and the last thing they want is to be singled out and treated differently. But at the same time they do want teachers to understand.

One student comments:

So maybe don't give an adopted person extra attention but just be more aware, subtly, in the background, that they may need a chat afterwards or they may need to come and see you or they may exhibit challenging behaviour. I think a lot of adopted people, including myself, do exhibit challenging behaviour. They're not – well, I wasn't – trying to be deliberately difficult. I just couldn't help it. So try to see through the behaviour.

In terms of potentially difficult curriculum issues and their impact on adopted students, another young woman said that teachers should ask the student how they feel rather than making assumptions:

Teachers shouldn't just assume it is an issue for them if they don't actually know. It would come across that the teacher is kicking a student out of the class when the student has no issue about what's going on in the class.

(Young people speaking as part of the Coram Adoptables schools project)

Exam pressure is stressful for most children but often constitutes an added burden for adopted children who have experienced trauma and attachment difficulties. Many adoptive parents, having seen how anxious and distressed their children are at school, would unhesitatingly prioritise emotional well-being over good exam results.

A list to identify "high need" students for teachers

In secondary schools, there are many different members of staff and the teachers cannot know every child personally. One way for a school to address this is to provide a "high need" list of students with photos and strategies given to all school staff so that they do not escalate a situation unwittingly because they do not know that child's needs.

A student "passport"

Some schools provide a "passport" for certain adopted children so that they can present it to different staff at the start of the lesson to tell them what is helpful or not helpful for them – for instance, a child may feel extremely anxious about what is going on behind them and may be able to settle only when they are sitting at the back of the class and able to see the door.

Communicating with your child's secondary school

For parents too, the transition to secondary school can take some adjustment. In primary school, there is one class teacher whom you can get to know and who can get to know you. When your child starts secondary school, it means you will have a new type of relationship with the school. The quick exchanges you may have had with teachers and other staff at the primary school gate will be a thing of the past.

If you want to speak to your child's form tutor, the designated teacher or any other teacher, you need to get in touch with the school by phone or email to find out when the teacher would be available. Teachers have a full schedule and you will need to make an appointment to have a chat with them.

Some schools arrange an EPAC (Chapter 6), which is similar to the PEP for children in care.

A home school agreement

Most secondary schools have a home school agreement to be signed by the school, the parent/carer and the child. This will include elements such as being respectful to one other, attending on time and following school rules. They are the expectations that each person should have of each other... If your child is being disciplined for reasons related to his difficulties in coping with the school and classroom environment, ask for a discussion initially with a member of staff such as the class teacher, form tutor or designated teacher.

(Alix and Fisher, forthcoming)

If communication starts breaking down

PAC-UK's advice line is sometimes able to offer advice to parents if communication has broken down between them and the school.

Helen Hoban of PAC-UK says their telephone advisers can help parents feel empowered to approach the school and also discuss with them how to have an effective conversation:

Sometimes it's helping them to stop and reflect and reassess how they might go in and address the issue. We have a lot on our website that they can share with the school, case studies, easily accessible information. If a school is not able to give a lot of time then pointing them to a clear, concise information leaflet is sometimes helpful to just say, 'I see, it makes sense, let's talk some more.'

(Helen Hoban, personal communication)

Sometimes either schools or parents (or both) can't understand what the difficulty is or where it comes from, she says.

> *Communication breaks down because people from either side can feel like they are banging their head against a brick wall. But getting people in a room to discuss what the underlying issues are, what the real frustrations are and starting to unpick them can be really powerful.*

(Helen Hoban, as above)

Parents might want to ask another professional from outside the school to come and support them in a meeting with the school.

For the celebrated author and adoptive mother Sally Donovan, the involvement of her adoption support social worker was critical when things were hanging in the balance for her son at secondary school.

'How social worker and teacher combined to turn around my adopted son's education'

One hot and sticky afternoon, almost exactly four years ago, Mr D and I and our social worker, our adopted son Jamie's teaching assistant and several members of his secondary school's leadership team settled awkwardly around a big table in a small meeting room. It wasn't called a crisis meeting but, looking back, that's what it was.

My heart was going like the clappers because I knew there was so much at stake. We were on the verge of dreadfulness. This was the end of the first year in secondary school and things were unravelling, at school and at home. A child who had coped well at primary school was hyper-vigilant, unable to focus and behaving inappropriately. Our family was barely hanging on and school were wobbling over whether this was the right place for Jamie. It could all have gone disastrously.

It didn't go disastrously. Four years on and our son is at the same school, is about to sit GCSEs and has his prom suit hanging in his wardrobe. Our family has weathered some extraordinary times and is doing well. So what changed?

Looking back, there were two critical people at that meeting, without whom things could have turned out very differently.

Having a knowledgeable and skilled social worker alongside us shifted things considerably. He spoke with experience and knowledge about trauma, why it is present in some children, how it's not a choice and why trying to threaten, train or exclude it away can make things worse.

He was able to suggest workable and flexible strategies that could be managed within the existing organisation, such as Jamie being able to leave the classroom, with no sanction, and seek safety in the student support centre.

Having a social worker say those things is far more powerful than a parent saying them. It sounds more like common sense and less like excuses.

*Sat quietly at that table was the newly appointed head of year. She listened carefully and borrowed a book I had brought along (*Inside I'm Hurting *by Louise Bomber). The following term she rang me from a course she was attending on supporting looked after and adopted children in school, run by Louise, to tell me how much sense it was all making and the ideas she had for supporting not just our adopted son, but many other children in school.*

The stream of detentions and letters home dried up, further training was carried out, triggers were identified, regular meetings took place, nerves were held and relationships were built.

Relationships were built and that really is the heart of it.

Relationships have been built between Jamie and the staff supporting him and looking out for him and they've been built between school and home.

These relationships are grounded in mutual respect, kind honesty and continual adjustment and learning, and they have given us all the resilience to get through some difficult times.

Over these four years the strategies and approaches put into place have improved feelings of safety and belonging. There hasn't been too much emphasis on academic learning, but rather on growing social and emotional skills while maintaining carefully chosen boundaries. Developing reflective skills has been particularly helpful, as has generally being made to feel welcome and valued at school. The learning is coming now, in great leaps, just ahead of the school finish line.

Raising children who see the world through the prism of trauma and shattered attachments can be a lonely and isolating business, particularly when the overwhelming narrative around schools can tend towards strong discipline, zero tolerance and no excuses. Our family have been lucky to have had the opportunity to build a relationship with a school prepared to work flexibly and with heart. This has enabled a young person who was dealt a tough hand to flourish.

There have been times along the way when success has been in the balance and that meeting four years ago was one of those times. What tipped the scales in the right direction was a skilled social worker and a school leadership willing to engage and to lead from the top.

(Donovan, 2016)

PAC-UK workers can suggest to parents how communication with the school might be more effective:

We can advise on types of conversations they might have, language they might want to use, questions they might want to raise. A lot of parents have already faced a number of struggles and assume it's going to go wrong when they go to the school... it's about how we build up their confidence to go back into the school and not go in all armoured up. We're not trying to encourage that at all – we are trying to help them feel empowered to go in to advocate for their child, to know what they can and can't ask and to know effective ways they can ask those questions in a way that the school will be able listen to and hear. It's about going in with clear points and knowing your aims before you go into the meeting, depending on what the issue is.

If a parent tells us: 'My child keeps getting detentions night after night, again and again and again, and the school are not listening when I say this isn't fair' – or maybe they haven't even had that conversation yet – we might suggest having a conversation along the lines of: 'I understand that the school has rules and policies but I'd like to understand where these detentions are coming from and how can we support my child' and perhaps asking: 'Is this detention the most effective way to help rebuild or re-work the behaviour?'

Parents can help the school to see things they have been missing. Sometimes in secondary school children get detention from one teacher and another and another, but it's actually all for the same thing. You can then spot a pattern and you can say 'Well, detention is clearly not addressing that

*behaviour so let's look at what else we can do that might be more effective'
and ask the school to think about some other ideas.*

(Helen Hoban, personal communication)

Adolescence and the teenage years

Much of what you have read in previous chapters applies to children and young people of all ages, up to starting in secondary school.

But secondary schools are very different from primary – and adolescents and teenagers are very different from younger children, so the road tends to get bumpier, if it hasn't already. The social pressures in adolescence and the teenage years are greater, there is more academic pressure, their behaviour can become more extreme and, of course, the stakes are higher.

The brain of an adolescent will not be mature for some years yet, and extensive brain re-development is still taking place, especially in the areas that deal with controlling impulses and complex social behaviour.

The influence of a child's peer group grows stronger and stronger as he or she gets into the teenage years, and the influence of parents appears to wane. It's the age-old struggle as the adolescent tries to separate from the parents and become more independent while parents can see that their child still needs some boundaries and protection (sometimes protection from themselves). Conflict is often a part of these years.

Don't give up trying to communicate with your child. You might find that, at times, teachers she likes and respects can get through to her better than you can, and other adults from outside the immediate family might be able to exert a positive influence.

In some adoptive families, these turbulent times are even more challenging. Children who have experienced trauma can sometimes feel drawn to others who have too, or who have emotional and behavioural challenges of their own, leading them to get into friendship groups involved in antisocial and offending behaviour. They may self-medicate with alcohol and drugs to dull the pain of traumatic memories, loss, grief and unknown pasts.

The issue of child-to-parent violence is becoming more widely recognised. In some adoptive families, children and adolescents are verbally abusive and controlling and even physically violent towards their parents; as they become bigger and stronger, their behaviour becomes even more difficult to cope with. Marriages and family relationships can collapse under the strain. Adoptions sometimes break down.

Adoption UK and PAC-UK are working with the DfE on a child-to-parent violence project (2017–2018) to train professionals and provide a range of interventions, services and support for parents, including an approach called 'non-violent resistance'. The project will be rolled out to local authorities, regional adoption agencies and adoptive parents. You may find this helpful if you are in this distressing situation (for more information, see www.pac-uk.org/cpv).

Some of the challenging issues facing teenagers (and their parents) are unfortunately well beyond the scope of this book. Don't forget that you can ask your local authority for post-adoption support for your child or family at any time – even if you've never asked for it before. This includes asking for an assessment of your needs. You may also wish to apply to the ASF (see Chapter 2) for funding for specialist therapy, for example therapeutic life story work.

Coming to terms with adoption

Adolescence is also a time when children begin to think about deeper questions in more abstract ways and questions of identity come to the fore. It's well known that the teenage years can be a time of existential angst and emotional intensity, but of course adopted children have even more complex feelings to grapple with than their peers.

In primary school I told everyone [that I was adopted] because I didn't really know what it meant, it was just something that made me "me". And just as someone will say, 'Oh, I live in London' I'd go, 'Oh, I live in London, I'm adopted' and people would go 'Oh, all right'. And then I hit sort of the teenage years and I thought, this is awful, I am so ashamed. No one understands. And due to that and, like, a number of different factors, I went slightly off the rails and made some poor choices. But no-one really knew how it felt and no-one could really empathise. Particularly my friends, they completely didn't understand. So that wasn't great. But then when people began to realise that my challenging behaviour was to do with adoption and they gave me more time of day, it got a lot easier. So patience and the teachers listening really helped.

(Young woman, speaking as part of the Coram Adoptables schools project)

Adolescence is a time when curiosity about birth parents increases and deepens, and sometimes becomes an unstoppable force. Parents need to give more detailed explanations to their child of why she had to be adopted and what their birth parents were like, and to make sure these explanations are not simplistic as they were in the early years, but appropriate to the child's greater understanding of human behaviour and social issues.

As we know all too well, some children and teenagers decide to search online for information or to find their birth family members – often without any support, mediation or safeguards and sometimes without the knowledge of their adoptive parents. This has been covered extensively elsewhere (e.g. in this author's 2013 book *Facing up to Facebook: A survival guide for adoptive parents*) and again is beyond the scope of this book.

However, parents and teachers should perhaps reflect on how issues of wondering about, searching for – and sometimes also contacting, possibly in secret – birth parents and other relatives can become the focus of a child's thinking. There are tragic and distressing events to somehow get your head around. This preoccupation can understandably interfere with a child's or young person's ability to concentrate on schoolwork and homework.

Basically being adopted is hard. It's like, you have lots of stuff to think about and you might not sleep at night because you're thinking about it. You know, like also you want to meet your parents, but... I'm trying to meet my family but my mum's just drinking and stuff. So I'm like – well, I could put it off but eventually I want to meet her, I mean, she's my mum. And just imagine having eight children took away from her...so... I take pity on her, but also – well, there's not a nice way to say it, basically.

(Young man, speaking as part of the Coram Adoptables schools project)

Peer pressure and bullying about adoption can intensify in these years. Friendships can be volatile and change overnight into enmity.

From a personal point of view, questions don't hurt. But jokes and rumours and speaking behind your back really do. So...if you have a problem, or if you have a question, ask me – and if I don't want to speak about it, please respect that. But often I probably will. And if I do trust you with that information, it's because I've liked you or trusted you, so don't then exploit that.

(Young woman, speaking as part of the Coram Adoptables school project)

Sadly, some adopted children are bullied in school or online, while others are simply left out – not included in games or invited to parties. It goes without saying that these situations can be heartbreaking for children and parents alike.

At the age of seven I showed my best friend my life story book and we fell out a week later and she shouted at me: 'At least I'm not adopted!' That made me wary. I had a difficult start to secondary school. Friends didn't include me, they were nasty to me and I kept my feelings bottled up. When I did tell my mum I was moved to another form and I found a new group of friends but I still didn't feel I fitted in. I still struggle to trust people but I've got more confidence since meeting my boyfriend.

(Cody, an adopted young person speaking at Adoption UK conference, 2017)

I was not bullied but I was isolated. The continual questions about my birth mother wore me down. The teacher didn't support me.

(Megan, an adopted young person speaking at Adoption UK conference, 2017)

Report any bullying or abuse to the school (keep a record of any abusive or offensive emails or messages and make sure your child knows not to reply). The school should be ready to deal with it robustly. It will have a policy on bullying – hold it to account. If the first person you report it to does not act, escalate it up the school management team.

In some secondary schools discipline leaves a lot to be desired, sexual harassment is rife and there are even incidences of sexual violence between children and young people. The Government has issued advice for schools and colleges on how to deal with this, covering:

- what sexual violence and harassment is;
- schools' and colleges' legal responsibilities;
- a whole school or college approach to safeguarding and child protection;

- how to respond to reports of sexual violence and sexual harassment.

(See https://www.gov.uk/government/publications/sexual-violence-and-sexual-harassment-between-children-in-schools-and-college)

Find out more about dealing with bullying at:
https://www.gov.uk/bullying-at-school/the-law

Anti-bullying Alliance
http://www.anti-bullyingalliance.org.uk/

Bullying UK
http://www.bullying.co.uk/general-advice/
0800 800 2222

Kidscape
https://www.kidscape.org.uk/
020 7730 3300

Social networking

The immense popularity of social networking as early as primary school is proving problematic for schools and parents alike. It has led to a rise in bullying as well as less obvious emotional risks to children's well-being. The media generally, including online media, can have a damaging effect on girls' body image and self-esteem, leaving them feeling that they don't match up to the ideal of being "thin" with which they are constantly bombarded. Looking at others' social media profiles can leave young people feeling that everyone else is more popular and having a much better time than they are. Children and young people can be left feeling disturbed by some of the violent and explicit videos they may see online. And watching online pornography can produce skewed and unrealistic ideas about sex, relationships, and how girls would like to be treated.

Some schools are taking the step of banning mobile phones in school because of the distraction and aggravation caused by young people using them for social networking in school. Even in primary school issues of online safety are important – and even if your child doesn't have a smartphone and you always supervise them at home when they are using the computer, their friends may well be showing them or introducing them to things that you would rather they did not see and were not aware of just yet.

The impact on children's lives of the internet and social networking is something that schools are increasingly having to deal with.

Parent Zone carried out a survey entitled 'The Perfect Generation: Is the internet undermining young people's mental health?' They interviewed young people and teachers and looked in-depth at the experiences of schools. This was the situation as seen by one school:

The internet and technology are identified here as factors exacerbating an already worrying situation. This school has seen pupils turn to the internet for affirmation, finding negativity or cruelty instead. They worry about pupils' inability to switch off from technology and desire to stay 'in the loop', making them unable to take a break from social drama even when they are in their own bedrooms. They feel that their pupils are unable to find a balance between online and offline without reliable adult guidance.

They have dealt with students looking up "dark" content about suicide and self-harm, but have also been troubled by worried young people turning to the internet for answers and coming back with unhelpful self-diagnoses. On the other hand, they have also started signposting some students in need of help to reputable websites, saying that much of the best available support is online. Again, they identify trusted adult guidance as the key in helping young people find helpful resources and avoid negative influences online.

A second school in the survey also reported problems spilling over from social media into the school:

This school does not blame the internet for pupil mental health, but they do feel their pupils sometimes use social media as a platform to be unkind.

For us, dealing with the aftermath when things go wrong, it's not the internet, it's social media. It's not the apps, it's what they do with them. They're mean to each other, they say mean things.

While this has always been a part of teenage life, with the rise of mobile devices, it's become continuous – their students have lost the ability to disconnect for the night at home.

They also see the internet as something that can validate negative behaviour, making bullying and nastiness seem acceptable because it's common and it's easy to do.

This school sees many parents struggling to enforce boundaries about internet use, making it more difficult for their children to manage online time. When parents do set rules, their children can be inadvertently isolated from their peers. One young male pupil feels he has been excluded by his friend group because he's not allowed to play 18-rated games with them outside of school. Each day they come in and discuss the games, leaving him on his own. It is difficult for well-meaning parents to find a balance between restricting inappropriate behaviour and socially disadvantaging their children.

These issues are also playing out with younger children, to the point where some pupils have "taken a step back" from technology by the time they are older. We heard that in this school, some teens even choose to come off social media because they don't want to deal with the negative side.

The effect of the internet on their pupils varies based on maturity levels, friendship groups and, in their view most importantly, home lives. In their experience, young people who have difficult relationships with their parents or whose parents are not willing to set boundaries about online time are more likely to experience problems.

(Rosen, 2016)

You cannot ban your child from the internet, though you may wish you could. The online world is a huge part of young people's lives. Many of them are only too well aware of the downsides of social networking, yet they are still prepared to put up with these in order to be able to enjoy the positives.

"Screen time" in itself is not necessarily bad for a child. Your child may be using the internet to research for homework, to collaborate on school projects, to find information on subjects she is interested in or to seek support from responsible websites. If a child is socially or geographically isolated, it can help them connect and keep in touch with friends at a distance.

But too much time spent online might mean that children and young people are spending less time interacting with friends face to face and enjoying physical activities like games and sport, which are good for their mood and fitness.

And children spending any amount of time online do need to learn how to stay safe, both to protect themselves from people who might pose risks of various kinds and to avoid getting into trouble through their own online activities. The more time they spend online, the higher the risk.

Your child may be more able than you to understand and use the technology but she is not necessarily emotionally mature enough to be able to cope with online risks and online interaction with other people.

There is a well-known disinhibiting effect of being behind a screen – people do and say things that they wouldn't do face to face. This can get people into trouble – teenagers, in particular, are more likely to act impulsively and less likely to anticipate risks. Indeed, some may actively seek out risk for the thrill of it.

Parents need to recognise the risks: children can easily be exposed to online pornography, hate content, violent and disturbing images and video, fake news, scams, sexting and live streaming, revenge porn, online grooming, gambling sites, cyberbullying, pro-anorexia and pro-suicide websites. Addiction to online games can be is another trap, with some spending so long on their screens that it interferes with eating, sleeping, socialising and schoolwork.

Online gaming or social networking into the early hours can leave young people feeling unable to "switch off", not getting enough sleep and consequently finding it hard to get to school and concentrate on lessons the next day.

Adopted young people who have difficulty forming friendships with their peers may be so keen to have friends that they are indiscriminately accepting of anyone who approaches them online. This can get them into trouble if they begin communicating with people who are out to exploit, bully or cause harm to others. Some children and young people end up being blackmailed and sexually exploited by people they have met online when they have gone along with their requests because they are keen to please and to make friends.

In some schools sexting is rife – young people see it as the norm. Girls are routinely asked to send explicit photographs of themselves. These can sometimes end up being circulated around the school and even more widely online. The child's school should help parents deal with this. If the image has been shared with other pupils, the school should have a process for dealing with it and will be able to help stop the image from being shared further. Social media sites should remove images like this if asked and the Internet Watch Foundation can work to get the picture removed from the internet.

The Internet Matters website has listed some of parents' most common concerns. It has advice about how to address these, along with advice on setting controls, filters and privacy settings and much more:

- My child spends too long on their smartphone/tablet.

- My child has been sexting.

- My child has shared their personal information on social media.

- My child has a social media account but they are under 13.

- My child is using numerous social media platforms and I am not sure how to keep them safe.

- My child has been groomed online.

- My child is a cyberbully.

- My child is being cyberbullied.

- My child has seen porn online.

- My child is self-harming.

- My child has been radicalised online.

- Other people are posting pictures of my child online without permission.

(See www.internetmatters.org/hub/expert-opinion-child-online-safety-addressing-top-parental-concerns.)

Keep the lines of communication open (as far as is possible with a teenager, though this is rarely easy). Make sure you have two-way communication – if it feels like a lecture, your child will zone out. Try to ask and listen as much as you speak. Be genuinely interested in what she is doing. It won't be all bad!

Reassure her that you won't blame her or be cross if bad stuff happens to her online – that way, your child will be more likely to tell you or ask for help if she gets into difficulties.

It can seem overwhelming and some parents are tempted to give up and just let their child get on with it, but this is a really important part of parenting. Even if you are not technologically skilled you can still show your child that you are concerned about what they are doing online and that you want to be "present" in their online life. That means talking with your child, often, about what they and their friends do online – taking an interest and discussing with them some of the difficult issues and things that can happen and asking how they would deal with them. It means setting rules and boundaries and ensuring young people have information and awareness that will help keep them safe.

There's no doubt it is a scary time to be a parent but there is a huge amount of information and advice about how to help your child or teenager to stay safe online. Educate yourself by reading the advice on the websites below, among others. Encourage your child to explore the e-safety sites – most of them have sections suitable for children of different ages, from very young children to teenagers, with games, quizzes, videos and other relatable information. Look at them together.

Here are a few to start off with:
www.childnet.com
www.internetmatters.org
www.thinkuknow.co.uk
www.saferinternet.org.uk
www.parentzone.org.uk

'How we feel as adopted young people in school'

We end this book with the views of a group of adopted teenagers taking part in the AT-ID project in Yorkshire and Humberside (www.at-id.org.uk). They want their teachers and support staff to know that:

- *We want you to stop making snap judgements about our behaviour, and instead ask us what would help.*

- *We need support rather than punishment; someone to talk to and listen, who can help us deal with our emotions.*

- *We want you to have training from specialists to help you understand why we sometimes get anxious, sad, feel mixed up, empty, confused, angry and lonely.*

- *We want adoption to be out in the open so we feel we can talk about it, rather than feeling ashamed or bottling it up.*

- *We need you to stop the bullying by improving how you tackle it.*

- *We want to learn about fostering and adoption in the same way that we learn about LGBT issues and other cultures and religions.*

- *We want help to meet other adopted teenagers; there are probably others like us in school but we don't know who they are.*

Key points

- The transition to secondary can be daunting, even for children who aren't adopted. As with starting primary, prepare your child as much as you can, including talking about it with her and taking her to visit the school.

- Be aware of the additional challenges such as new classmates, many more teachers, new subjects, higher expectations, greater noise, etc, all of which are potential triggers for adopted children.

- Make sure you know the key people, such as the designated teacher or form tutor, so that you can arrange to discuss any concerns with them.

- Watch out for peer pressure and bullying, both of which can intensify in adolescents; sadly, adopted children can seem like an easy target. Ask the school to take action straight away if your child is being bullied.

- Consider the quality and effect of your child's use of screen time and especially social networking. Talk to her about the use of privacy settings and how to stay safe online.

References

Adoption UK (2017) *Adopted Children 20 Times More Likely to be Excluded,* Banbury: Adoption UK.

Alix S and Fisher A (forthcoming) *The Foster Carers' Handbook on Education: Getting the best for your child,* London: CoramBAAF.

Bath & North East Somerset Council/National College for Teaching and Leadership (2014) *An Introduction to Attachment and the Implications for Learning and Behaviour.* Available at: www.bathspa.ac.uk/media/bathspaacuk/education-/research/digital-literacy/education-resource-introduction-to-attatchment.pdf.

Bentley CB (2013) Great expectations: supporting 'unrealistic' aspirations for children in care. In Jackson S (ed.) *Pathways through Education for Young People in Care,* London: BAAF, pp. 45–52.

Bergin C and Bergin D (2009) 'Attachment in the classroom', *Educational Psychology Review 21,* pp. 141–170.

Bomber L (2007) *Inside I'm Hurting: Practical strategies for supporting children with attachment difficulties in schools,* Duffield: Worth Publishing.

Bradbury A and Roberts-Holmes G (2017) *Grouping in Early Years and Key Stage 1: "A necessary evil"?,* London: UCL Institute of Education. Available at: https://neu.org.uk/sites/neu.org.uk/files/NEU279-Grouping-in-early-years-KS1.PDF.

Brown J (2015) 'The challenges of caring for a child with FASD'. *Adoption & Fostering,* 39(3), pp. 247–255.

Burnell A (2017) 'Therapeutic approach to education for adopted children in mainstream schools', *Family Futures.* Available at: www.familyfutures.co.uk/therapeutic-approach-education-needed-adopted-children-mainstream-schools.

Coram Life Education (film). www.coramlifeeducation.org.uk/adoptables/.

Department for Education (December 2014a) *Advice on the Admission of Summer Born Children for Local Authorities, School Admission Authorities and Parents*. Available at: www.gov.uk/government/uploads/system/uploads/attachment_data/file/389448/Summer_born_admissions_advice_Dec_2014.pdf.

Department for Education (December 2014b) *School Admissions Code: Statutory guidance for admission authorities, governing bodies, local authorities, schools adjudicators and admission appeals panels.* Available at: www.gov.uk/government/publications/school-admissions-code--2.

Department for Education (March 2018) *School Exclusions Review:Terms of reference*. Available at: www.gov.uk/government/publications/school-exclusions-review-terms-of-reference.

Department for Education (February 2018) *The Designated Teacher for Looked-after and Previously Looked-after Children: Statutory guidance on their roles and responsibilities*. Available at: www.gov.uk/government/publications/designated-teacher-for-looked-after-children.

Donovan S (2016) 'How social worker and teacher combined to turn around my son's education', *Community Care*, 18 May.

Donovan T (2017) 'Two-thirds of schools without mental health champion', *Children & Young People Now*, 21 December. Available at: www.cypnow.co.uk/cyp/news/2004664/two-thirds-of-schools-without-mental-health-champion.

Fursland E (2013) *Facing Up to Facebook: A survival guide for adoptive families*, London: CoramBAAF.

Geddes H (2006) *Attachment in the Classroom: The links between children's early experience, emotional wellbeing and performance in school*, Duffield: Worth Publishing. Cited in Bath & North East Somerset Council/National College for Teaching and Leadership, as above, p. 14.

Guest S (2018) *Pupil Premium: Why it can sometimes be difficult to get the right support for adopted children in schools*. Available at: https://educationandadoption.wordpress.com/2018/03/14/pupil-premium-why-it-can-sometimes-be-difficulut-to-get-the-right-support/.

Hughes D (2012) *Parenting a Child with Emotional and Behavioural Difficulties*. London: BAAF.

Jackson C (2017) *Working in the NHS: The state of children's services*, Lutterworth, Leicestershire: British Association for Counselling and Psychotherapy.

John B (2017) 'The big decision', *SEN Magazine*, Sept–Oct, Issue 90.

Local Government and Social Care Ombudsman (2017 *'A disproportionate burden'- families struggling with new special educational needs system when councils get it wrong.* Available at: www.lgo.org.uk/information-centre/news/2017/oct/a-disproportionate-burden-families-struggling-with-new-special-educational-needs-system-when-councils-get-it-wrong.

Marshall N (2018) 'Focusing on attachment', *SEN Magazine*, 8 January. Available at: https://senmagazine.co.uk/home/uncategorised/focussing-on-attachment.

Mather M (2018) *Dealing with Foetal Alcohol Spectrum Disorder: A guide for social workers*, London: CoramBAAF.

Nock J (undated) 'In a class of their own', *SEN Magazine,* 30 May. Available at: https://senmagazine.co.uk/home/articles/senarticles-2/in-a-class-of-their-own.

NOFAS-UK (2017) *Teaching a Student with FASD*. Available at: www.nofas-uk.org/TeachingAStudentWithFASD_FIN%20REV.pdf.

OECD (Organisation for Economic Co-operation and Development) (2014) *Education Indicators in Focus*. Available at: www.oecd.org/edu/skills-beyond-school/.

Rees Centre (2017) *Principles for the Alex Timpson Programme on Attachment and Trauma in Schools*, Research Programme. Information available at: http://reescentre.education.ox.ac.uk/research/alex-timpson-attachment-and-trauma-programme-in-schools/.

Rees Centre (2018) *Evaluations of Attachment Aware Schools Programmes*, Report. Available at: http://reescentre.education.ox.ac.uk/research/evaluation-of-attachment-aware-schools/.

Roberts B (2015) ' "I know that I'm in my own world; it's ok, they know me here": the challenge of coping with FASD in educational settings', *Adoption & Fostering*, 39(3), pp. 235–246.

Rosen R (2016) '"The Perfect Generation": Is the internet undermining young people's mental health?', *Parent Zone*. Available at: https://parentzone.org.uk/sites/default/files/The%20Perfect%20Generation%20report.pdf.

Treisman K (2017) *Working with Relational and Developmental Trauma in Children and Adolescents*, Oxford: Routledge.

Walter S (2016) 'Early experiences in the neurosequential model in education', *The Canadian Journal for Teacher Research*. Available at: www.teacherresearch. ca/blog/article/2016/10/30/314-early-experiences-in-the-neurosequential-model-in-education.

Blogs and websites

Anonymous (2017). *How my brain works.*
Available at: https://allaboutmyuniquelife.wordpress.com/.

AT-ID (a project for adopted teenagers from 11 to 18 years old who live in the Yorkshire and Humberside area. See: www.at-id.org.uk.

Blogfox14, A. p. w. a. (2017) *Adoption: The Bear Facts.*
Available at: https://adoptionthebearfacts.wordpress.com.

Newby C (2016) *The Newby Tribe.* Available at: https://thenewbytribe.com/ adoption/safeguarding-adopted-children-in-school/.

SB-FASD (29 April 2017) *The Same Child Shines When Seen Through a Different Prism*, FASDLearningWithHope.wordpress.com. Available at: https://fasdlearningwithhope.wordpress.com/2017/04/29/same-child/.

Useful resources

Where parents and schools can get information, advice, training and support with education issues

Adoption UK

Adoption UK is a national charity and network for adoptive parents, with over 10,000 members.

Adoption UK has done a great deal of research and campaigning around education and offers training, consultation and a wide range of resources for adoptive parents. Adoption UK has joined forces with the National Association of Head Teachers (NAHT), and others, in a bid to make every school attachment-aware. The aim of the Schools Campaign is to provide all school leaders and teachers with knowledge, practical strategies, access to training, and a network of support through Adoption UK's schools' membership programme.

Adoption UK offers a range of support services for adopters, including advice, information, an online forum, peer support and adopters' groups around the country.

www.adoptionuk.org
@AdoptionUK and @AUK_Schools

Trauma-Informed Schools UK

www.traumainformedschools.co.uk
Beacon House
@BeaconHouseTeam

Attachment-Aware Schools

This is a partnership between Bath Spa University, the National College for Teaching and Leadership, the virtual schools of Bath & North East Somerset and Stoke on Trent and the training organisation Kate Cairns Associates (led by attachment specialist Kate Cairns) and schools. It trains teachers, heads and school governors to be "attachment-aware".

Attachment-Aware Schools says:

There is a body of information and research available to specialist practitioners, like social care and mental health staff, that we want to share with the teachers and school support workers who make a difference every day in schools and early years settings.

So far we have brought together schools, other settings and their partner agencies with specialist trainers. Together, the aim of the work has been to create "attachment-aware" schools and communities in which all children and young people experience the nurturing environments they need to grow and achieve.

On its website, there are resources from the Attachment-Aware Schools training programme and a list of trainers and organisations that are able to work with schools to develop greater attachment awareness. All the materials are informed by research and based on evidence from classroom practice.

www.attachmentawareschools.com

Emotion coaching

Emotion coaching is an approach used to support children and young people with their behaviour and mental and emotional well-being. It emphasises the importance of considering the emotions underlying behaviours "in the moment" before dealing with setting limits and solving problems.

The aim is to de-escalate difficult situations, increase children's and young people's understanding of their emotions and support their emotional regulation.

It involves five steps in this order: tuning in, connecting, listening, reflecting and problem-solving.

Some schools have introduced emotion coaching as a peer mentoring programme, with selected older pupils being trained to use it with younger pupils.

Emotion coaching was developed by Professor John Gottman in the USA and there is research on it from England, the USA and Australia. It helps children to explore their feelings and relationships, to reflect with others and deal with their core emotions such as anger, fear and anxiety rather than projecting them through challenging behaviour.

It is one of the techniques used by schools that are working towards becoming "attachment-aware".

For further information, see www.emotioncoaching.co.uk and www.attachmentawareschools.com

FAGUS

FAGUS (Fostering Attachment Awareness to Generate Understanding in Schools) is a framework for measuring the attainment of goals for children in areas that fall outside the academic curriculum.

It is a resource for assessing, monitoring and supporting children's emotional and social development and measuring their progress in these areas. It was developed at Beech Lodge School in Berkshire, a specialist independent school that caters for children who have attachment- and trauma-related difficulties, many of whom are adopted (see below). Other schools can buy the resource to use with particular children who are having difficulties.

It outlines the developmental processes in a child's social and emotional development across 13 different domains, which include: awareness and understanding of others; self-control; motivation and self-efficacy; and moral development. This allows you to identify at what age level a child is functioning and his or her strengths and weaknesses across each domain.

Teachers can then focus specific interventions to encourage social and emotional progress and measure the child's success.

www.fagus.org.uk
@FagusResource

Beech Lodge School

This is a small, attachment-focused independent special school in Berkshire for children aged from seven to 18. It provides an alternative educational experience for children who have needs that are difficult to meet in a conventional school setting.

www.beechlodgeschool.co.uk
@beechlodge

FASD Network UK

Consultancy on individual children, training for professionals, support groups for families in the north-east and North Yorkshire, and free downloadable resources for teachers and caregivers.

www.fasdnetwork.org

NOFAS-UK (National Organisation for Foetal Alcohol Syndrome) UK

Provides information, training and resources for people affected by FASD, their parents, carers and professionals. The organisation has some useful resources for teachers and teaching assistants. It will also try to help parents who call with queries about children's education.

http://www.nofas-uk.org/

Inner world work

This is an online resource centre for parents and carers, offering a collection of free, high quality resources to support parents, carers and children who are trauma-experienced. These include information sheets on What survival looks like in primary school, What survival looks like in secondary school, and the Whole Class Happy Pack of practical, easy, free, grounding and relaxation ideas for teachers to use on a daily basis to create a safer, happier classroom environment. The campaign is run by a group of parents in West Sussex.

www.innerworldwork.co.uk
@InnerWorldWork

IPSEA

The Independent Parental Special Education Advice (known as IPSEA) offers free and independent legally based information, advice and support to help get the right education for children and young people with all kinds of special educational needs and disabilities. IPSEA gives advice and support on:

- local authorities' legal duties to assess and provide for children with special educational needs;

- exclusions of children with special needs/disabilities;

- action/inaction by local authorities and/or schools which discriminate against children and young people with disabilities.

www.ipsea.org.uk
@IPSEAcharity

Nurture groups

Nurture groups are an intervention used with vulnerable and disadvantaged children and young people and those who have social, emotional and behavioural difficulties, for instance, those who are withdrawn or aggressive, have low self-esteem, are disengaged from learning, or who won't stay in the classroom.

They are in-school classes of six to 12 children or young people in early years settings or primary or secondary schools. Two teachers run the group, providing warmth, acceptance and nurturing experiences to help remove the barriers to the children's learning and help them develop positive relationships with teachers and peers. There is a lot of emphasis on communication and social learning. As well as regular lessons, activities include emotional literacy sessions, sharing news and eating breakfast together.

Children attend nurture groups often on a part-time basis but remain part of their main class group and usually return full-time to their own class within two to four terms.

Nurture groups are evidence-based, have been used in the UK for 40 years and are now in over 1,500 schools in the UK. They are also used in other countries, including Canada, New Zealand and Romania.

The most common way to fund nurture group provision in the UK is through the Pupil Premium.

www.nurturegroups.org
@nurturegroups

Mentally Healthy Schools

This website provides information, advice and resources to help primary schools understand and promote all children's mental health and well-being.

www.mentallyhealthyschools.org.uk

PAC-UK and Adoption-Friendly Schools training

PAC-UK offers:

- Training to schools in supporting children with histories of trauma and loss, as well as transitions, effective use of the Pupil Premium Plus and developing children's executive functioning skills.

- A six-day course for schools called Becoming an Adoption-Friendly School.

- Schools can buy in training sessions and consultations focussing on developing whole-school good practice or on specific children.

- PAC-UK has an Education Advice Line for adoptive parents, special guardians and school staff to talk through any school or educational concerns. (Wednesday and Thursdays, 10am–12 noon, excluding half-terms and holidays. Tel: 020 7284 5879 or email education@pac-uk.org).

- In some areas, PAC-UK's education and well being workers can offer therapeutic support in schools including running transition groups, mindfulness groups, friendship groups and so on for children and reflective practice groups for staff.

www.pac-uk.org
@PACUKadoption

The Adoptables

The Adoptables is a peer network of adopted young people aged 13 to 25, organised and run by Coram. With their help, Coram Life Education has produced a Schools Toolkit to teach pupils about adoption. The free Toolkit includes lesson plans, teachers' guidance, films and activities for Key Stages 2 and 3. Some of the Adoptables also go into schools to speak about their experiences as adopted young people.

www.coramlifeeducation.org.uk/adoptables/
@CoramAdoptables

Advice on school admission for summer-born children (and others whose parents feel they are not ready)

www.gov.uk/government/uploads/system/uploads/attachment_data/
file/389448/Summer_born_admissions_advice_Dec_2014.pdf

Attachment and trauma interventions and training for children, families and schools

Consultancies

Louise Michelle Bomber
TouchBase
www.touchbase.org.uk
@theyellowkite

Kate Cairns
Kate Cairns Associates
www.kca.training
@kcatraining

Nicola Marshall
Braveheart Education
www.bravehearteducation.co.uk
@BraveHeartEdu

Dr Jennifer Nock
www.jennifernocktrainingandconsultancy.com
@jennifer_nock

Dr Karen Treisman
Safe Hands and Thinking Minds Associates
www.safehandsthinkingminds.co.uk
@dr_treisman

Further reading

Inclusive Strategies to Support Pupils with Attachment Difficulties Make it through the School Day
Louise Michelle Bomber, 2011, Worth Publishing.

Inside I'm Hurting: Practical strategies for supporting children with attachment difficulties in schools
Louise Michelle Bomber, 2007, Worth Publishing.

Educating Children and Young People with Fetal Alcohol Spectrum Disorders
Carolyn Blackburn, 2012, Routledge.

Meeting the Needs of Adopted and Permanently Placed Children: A guide for adoptive parents, 2017, PAC-UK.

Meeting the Needs of Adopted and Permanently Placed Children: A guide for school staff
Julia Clements, 2017, Adoption UK.

Becoming an Adoption-Friendly School: A whole-school resource for supporting children who have experienced trauma or loss
Emma Gore-Langton and Katherine Boy, 2017, Jessica Kingsley Publishers.

Parenting Adopted Teenagers: Advice for the adolescent years
Rachel Staff, 2016, Jessica Kingsley Publishers.

Appendix

The education system: the basics

This section provides some basic information about the education system, for those who are new to it all. Much of the information is adapted from a companion book for foster carers (Alix and Fisher, forthcoming).

Personal Education Plans

All looked after children are required by law to have a Personal Education Plan (PEP) so, if you are adopting a child of school age, he or she will have a PEP in place. This outlines the child's developmental and educational needs and progress and will include short- and long-term targets, goals and aspirations. It is a tool to track a young person's progress and indicate ways of supporting their education. The PEP should be reviewed every six months.

The child's social worker is responsible for co-ordinating the plan and arranging the review meetings. The people who attend are:

- the looked after child;
- the social worker;
- the carer(s);
- the designated teacher (explained below).

Some schools also have Education Plans for Adopted Children, initiated when a looked-after child is adopted, provided the parents choose to identify their child as adopted. These work in a similar way to PEPs.

Who's who in the education system?

It helps if you understand the roles and responsibilities of the many different professionals in the education system and who to turn to for particular support or advice. The key people are:

The virtual school head teacher

A virtual school head teacher is an experienced teacher who works for a local authority, sometimes as part of a virtual school team. She or he is responsible for promoting and supporting the educational achievement of all children looked after by that local authority. While children each attend their own schools, they are listed on a "virtual" school roll or list.

As this book goes to press, the Department for Education has approved a grant to support local authorities in England to appoint virtual school heads for previously looked after children, providing details on the amount of funding awarded to each local authority for the 2018 to 2019 financial year and including a link to statutory guidance on the new role for virtual school heads supported by this funding (see www.gov.uk/government/publications/virtual-school-heads-section-31-grant-determination-letter).

Teachers

In primary school, each class has a main teacher who teaches a large range of subjects. This is likely to be your first point of contact for your child and she or he will probably get to know you and your child very well. Some primary schools employ specialist teachers to teach subjects such as PE or music. In a secondary school, the structure is different and your child will have a large number of teachers with specialist subject knowledge.

The designated teacher for looked after children/children adopted from care

All schools must have a designated teacher for looked after children. In many schools one person will fulfil the roles of both the designated teacher for looked after children and the designated person for previously-looked after children (i.e. adopted or under special guardianship). Sometimes this might be a head teacher, the deputy or the special educational needs co-ordinator (SENCO). It is the designated teacher's responsibility to support staff and make sure that everyone working with looked after adopted children understands the issues that might arise. They will work with other agencies, such as your child's social worker/your post-adoption support worker and the VSH. She or he should ensure that your child is getting the best from their school and seek ways to support them if needed.

The designated teacher for child protection

Each school will also have a designated teacher for child protection and safeguarding. This is normally the head teacher but may also include the deputy. They will have an overview of any safeguarding concerns of pupils within their school and teachers will go to them for advice if they are concerned about a particular child.

Education welfare officers

Education welfare officers work with schools, pupils, parents and carers to support regular attendance. They become involved with families when a child is failing to attend school at an expected level or is regularly late. They support families and identify difficulties that need attention.

Special educational needs co-ordinators (SENCOs)

All schools must have a SENCO. They will co-ordinate the extra support required for children with additional needs and disabilities and will work with parents and carers to discuss what this might be; for instance, small group sessions, interventions around a specific area of learning or one-to-one support. SENCOs also work closely with a wide range of other professionals such as educational psychologists, and speech and language or play therapists. The SENCO will also work with the class teacher to set a pupil targets for learning and discuss what support a child will need to achieve them. S/he will hold a meeting (normally each term) with the parent/carer and teacher to discuss the child's progress.

Pastoral support

Pastoral support is about promoting pupils' well-being. One approach is for the school to employ a learning mentor who helps pupils to deal with any individual difficulties or issues that that might affect their learning. Mentors may help with issues such as poor attendance, low self-esteem and confidence, behaviour or emotional difficulties, settling into a school, bereavement or problems at home. They may work with a pupil on a one-to-one basis or run small groups around a particular area, such as anger management.

Tutors

In secondary schools (and some middle schools), your child will have a tutor. She or he oversees a group of pupils and will meet them most days for the register and tutorial sessions that can become their form group. The tutor should get to know your child well, even though she or he may not teach them for a subject, especially if she or he stays involved with your child throughout their time in secondary school. If you have any concerns regarding your child in general or you have queries but are not sure whom to ask, then the tutor will be able to help or direct you.

Heads of year

In a secondary school, the head of year has an overview of the year group. They are likely to become involved in things like inclusion, attendance, bullying and serious incidents. If your child is having difficulties in several lessons, you should contact the head of year who can gather information to form an overview.

The team around the child

Schools work with many agencies and professionals. The "team around the child" comprises the group of professionals who work together to support individual children who are having difficulties or who have additional needs of one kind or another. The composition of the group will depend on the child's needs and may work around a plan that is in place. The team may work from a central base or from several places but come together for meetings as necessary.

The role of the governing body

The school's governing body is made up of the head and selected teachers, and may include parents and outsiders such as representatives from the local community. They are volunteers who are committed to support the school, pupils and staff, and to improve the school as much as possible. They can have a wide range of talents and abilities and may have known the school for a long time.

Their task is to ensure that the school delivers good quality education, hold the head teacher to account for the performance of the school, oversee financial aspects and ensure that money is well spent. They are also involved in hearing appeals and grievances, setting standards for behaviour and discipline and ensuring that pupils are safe.

The National Curriculum

Most schools teach the National Curriculum. It is not compulsory for independent schools or academies to do so, but most do.

The National Curriculum is a set of subjects outlining what pupils should be taught, and the standards they should reach in each subject. The subjects taught at primary school (Key Stages 1 and 2) are:

- English;
- maths;
- science;
- design and technology;
- history;
- geography;
- art and design;
- music;
- physical education (PE), including swimming;
- computing;
- a foreign language (at Key Stage 2).

Schools must also provide religious education (RE) and sex education – although parents/carers and guardians can ask for their children to be taken out of the whole lesson or part of it. Schools often also teach personal, social and health education (PSHE) and citizenship.

Compulsory sex and relationships education is due to be introduced in all secondary schools, and relationships education in all primaries, from 2019.

In secondary school, in Key Stage 3, pupils will study the above subjects but probably in more detail: for example, within design and technology they may specifically be taught textiles, food technology and resistant materials. Pupils are then able to select their options for Key Stage 4, but this will include English, maths and science. Some schools also make other subjects compulsory such as computing or a modern foreign language. Subjects beyond 16 years of age are more diverse: young people have the opportunity to study academic qualifications in the form of A-levels, diplomas and work-based training in the form of apprenticeships. New A-level subjects include areas such as dance and drama, criminology, electronics, film studies and world development.

Are there other options?

Some schools (such as private schools or academies) do not have to teach the National Curriculum and may choose to follow another programme instead. Whatever curriculum it is following, each school needs to demonstrate children's learning and progress. Private schools are inspected by the Independent Schools Inspectorate (ISI) and academies are subject to inspection by Ofsted to ensure that this is happening.

Teaching in groups

Children are taught within different teaching groups at school. Often in primary schools this is done in mixed-ability groups. In some subjects such as English and maths, children may be put into ability sets, in which those of higher, middle and lower abilities sit and work together. This means that the tasks they are set and support they receive in class meet their needs at the level at which they are currently working. Groups may change throughout the year depending on the topic area being taught and your child's and other children's progress within the group.

The teaching union, the National Education Union (NFU), has serious reservations about the effect of grouping in the early years of primary school. In a 2017 report (Bradbury and Roberts-Holmes, 2017), it found that grouping by "ability" or attainment is common in Key Stage 1 in primary schools in England, and takes many forms and says that these practices continue despite the research evidence that mixed ability teaching produces higher attainment overall. It says that teachers have concerns about the negative impact of grouping on children's confidence, self-esteem and aspirations potentially leading to mental health problems.

In secondary schools a system called "banding" is often used. This is where pupils are grouped broadly depending on their ability and then taught within these groups for most subjects like history, geography and science; sometimes English and maths are more specifically set.

Checking progress

Children are assessed in many different ways: set tasks, projects, verbal discussion, homework, tests and exams. These fit into two types of assessment: day-to-day feedback and progress checks.

Progress checks usually consist of a test or exam given at the end of a set piece of work, such as at the end of a half-term or school year. This includes SATs tests, GCSEs and A-levels. They also include "teacher assessments", perhaps where a teacher rather than someone from outside the school is observing a child with a task or marking his or her work. The aim is to assess the broad level a child has reached at a given time.

What should I expect my child to be tested on and when?

Below we have set out the testing regime at the time of writing, though it may have changed by the time you read this book. The current Government is proposing to scrap the Key Stage 1 SATs, tests which are opposed by many parents and teachers, though it plans to keep them in place until at least 2023. The current Government also proposes introducing new Baseline Assessment tests for reception children, which may include looking at children's "self-regulation".

- In Key Stage 1 (Year 1), a phonics screening test is carried out. This is where a child's ability to "decode" words for reading is assessed.

- At the end of Key Stage 1 (Year 2), national tests (SATs) and teacher assessments are carried out in English, maths and science.

- At the end of Key Stage 2 (Year 6), national tests (SATs) and teacher assessments are carried out in English and maths, and teacher assessments in science. Children aiming for a place at one of England's 164 grammar schools (set to increase under the current Government) take the Eleven-Plus.

- At the end of Key Stage 4 (Year 11), GCSEs take place.
- In addition, pupils are often tested throughout the year and at the end of each school year by the school.

Exams

Pupils will need to choose the subjects for their GCSEs. Some subjects will be compulsory, such as English and maths, and others they will be able to choose. Schools differ in what they require as compulsory subjects. For example, some schools will require all pupils to take a language, others will not. You and your child will be given further guidance in Year 9 and you will be invited to attend an options evening to discuss the subjects with your child and their teachers.

GCSEs

Expectations are that pupils will achieve five GCSEs grades A*–C including English and maths. The assessment of English and maths has been changed to a numerical system from 9 to 1 (9 being the highest grade). Pupils will now be expected to gain a level 4 or above.

A levels and other options

In Years 10 and 11, pupils will need to consider their next steps in education. The school will have a career guidance adviser and your child can meet with him or her to discuss options. You may want to explore Further Education and Higher Education colleges and apprenticeship schemes in addition to A-level options if your child is able to stay on in education.

Special educational needs

Many looked after and adopted children have some kind of special educational need. This term applies to those who need additional support and extra help.

You or your child's teacher may be worried if your child is not making enough progress. It may be specific areas such as in maths or reading and writing. As explained throughout this book, emotional or behavioural issues can get in the way of your child's learning and limiting his or her progress. Or it may be because your child has a physical need, and adjustments within the classroom or the use of specialist equipment are needed.

Additional support may include:

- a special learning programme, such as maths;
- a nurture group to support social skills;
- specialist equipment;
- extra support from an assistant;
- small group work;
- someone observing and supporting in class or at play and lunchtime;
- assistance in taking part in classroom activities;
- help communicating with other children;
- support with physical difficulties such as eating, changing for PE or using the toilet.

For children with a higher level of need who meet the threshold, an EHCP is put into place that may continue until a young person is 25 years of age (see Chapter 7) – www.gov.uk/children-with-special-educational-needs/extra-SEN-help).

School behaviour policies

In secondary schools sanctions may include detention during a break time, lunchtime or at the end of the day. If you would like further information on detentions, ask the school for a copy of their behaviour policy and speak to your child's form tutor or head of year if you would like to discuss the behaviour that is causing concern. Schools no longer need to give notice of an after-school detention; however, most schools do so to ensure that arrangements can be made for a child to get home safely afterwards. If behaviour issues escalate, then exclusion may be considered, and this is discussed further in Chapter 6.

Schools try to work with children to regulate their own behaviour, rather than to discipline them. For children who continually present challenging behaviour, a plan may have to be made which specifies the range of options for teachers to use along with the possibility of further professional support, such as referral to a behaviour support teacher who can support the child in school and/or at home.

Teachers are allowed to use reasonable force if necessary to remove a child from a classroom, or to prevent a child from leaving. Schools would, of course, avoid this if at all possible. (The use of force could have a serious impact on any child, let alone a child who has experienced trauma or violence.) Schools are also able to search pupils' bags to check that dangerous or illegal items are not brought into school.

Gifted and talented children

Some children are classed as "gifted" "talented" or "higher learning potential'". The term "gifted" tends to relate to academic subjects such as maths or history, whereas "talented" tends to apply to subjects such as PE or drama. Higher Learning Potential (HLP) is a commonly used phrase which incorporates any subject.

If your child is identified as having particular strengths in an area, then you may receive a letter from the school to let you know this. They may also have the opportunity to take part in additional activities, such as events with other school or trips with other children around a particular skill, such as leadership. The SENCO may oversee this group of children or the school may have a separate Gifted and Talented/HLP co-ordinator. Children who are Gifted and Talented fit within the term "inclusion" as they are overseen to ensure that they are challenged and reach their potential and are protected from any potential bullying because they stand out from others.

Schools and Key Stages

Infant, junior and primary schools

- Infant schools educate children from the ages of four until seven.

- Junior schools follow on from infant schools and provide for children aged seven to 11.

- Primary schools cover both age ranges under the same school, from four to 11 years.

- The first year of school is called the Reception year, and is for children aged four to five years old.

- Children then move into Year 1, followed by Year 2. This is known as Key Stage 1 (KS1).

- Children then move into Years 3, 4, 5 and 6. This is known as Key Stage 2 (KS2).

- In some schools, children may start school the term before they are five years old. Other schools have one entry point and all children start in the September of the school year in which they are five.

Middle schools

- In some parts of England, such as Suffolk and Dorset, there is a different school system that runs across the age ranges and this includes middle schools.

- The first school educates pupils aged four to eight years, the middle schools is for nine- to 13-year-olds, and the upper school teaches 14- to 16-year-olds.

- In some areas, middle schools are being phased out and replaced with the primary and secondary school system.

Secondary schools

- Secondary schools are for pupils aged 11 to 16 years old.

- Some pupils will stay at their secondary school to do A-levels at sixth form until they are 18 or 19 years old.

- Some will go to another school, may attend a further education college or may start an apprenticeship or another form of training when aged 16 years.

- In areas that still have grammar schools, admission to a grammar school is normally through an entrance exam that children take the year before. For information on grammar school entry, see your local authority guidance.

For information on different types of school (academies, free schools, private schools, faith schools, etc) visit the government website: www.gov.uk/types-of-school

Special schools and additional provision units

● Special schools include schools that have provision for children with additional needs or disabilities.

● Entrance into these schools will be through a child's Education and Health Care Plan (EHCP) as explained above.

● Pupils have more individualised support for their needs.

● Pupil Referral Units (PRUs) support children who do not attend mainstream school due to exclusion, behavioural needs or pregnancy.

● Many pupils at a PRU are "school refusers" or pupils who have been excluded, who find mainstream schools difficult.

● PRUs may offer part-time and full-time education.

● PRUs may be used as part of a short-term or longer-term plan.

Attendance

If you are having difficulty getting your child to attend, you should receive support from the school.

If your child has a health problem and is unable to attend for a long period of time, see www.gov.uk/illness-child-education for more information.

Holidays

You must get permission from the head teacher if you want to take your child out of school during term time. You need to apply to him or her in advance and you can be fined if you take them out of school without permission. For more information go to: www.gov.uk/education-attendance-council.

School uniform

Each school decides what its uniform will be and will have a policy on this. Children can be disciplined if the correct uniform is not worn. This may result in a detention or being sent home to change.

School reviews

Children who are looked after (including those in an adoptive placement before the adoption order is made) have reviews that happen around the PEP.

If your child has a special educational need, they are likely to have a further review, called a one-plan review. You will meet with your child's SENCO and class teacher once a term and discuss your child's progress against targets that have been set. You will also discuss any reports that have been sought from specialists who have been working with your child, such as a speech and language therapist. If your child is receiving any additional support in school, such as attending a nurture group or as part of an intervention group, then this will be reviewed to see how effective it is.

If your child has an EHCP, this will be reviewed annually with a member of a specialist team from the local authority.

Supporting children's education

School is a vital part of children's everyday life. But only 13% of children looked after by local authorities in England achieve the currently expected standard – five GCSE passes at grade 1–4. The gap in attainment widens with age.

Lack of qualifications puts these young men and women at a huge disadvantage. So what helps young people in care to do well, and what gets in the way? Here are some titles on education that focus on helping children to learn.

Pathways through Education for Young People in Care: Ideas from research and practice, Sonia Jackson (ed.). £19.95
Brings together evidence from inter-disciplinary research with innovations in practice that have been shown to make a world of difference both in the UK and overseas.

Learn the Child, Kate Cairns and Chris Stanway. £24.95
Explains why children and young people in care may do less well than their peers at all stages of education, due to their experiences of separation, loss and trauma; addresses behavioural issues and assists the reader to help traumatised children to learn.

Ten Top Tips on Supporting Education, Eileen Fursland with Kate Cairns and Chris Stanway. £9.95
Looks at the positive steps that social workers and carers can take to support the child, including assessing the impact of his or her history, forming a relationship with key school staff, supporting the child through transitions and ensuring that he or she has information that makes sense to them.

Supporting Children's Learning: A training programme for foster carers, Clare Pallett, John Simmonds and Andrea Warman. £20.00 +VAT
Helps carers to understand the processes involved in learning, create a conducive environment, and support and encourage the development of social and emotional skill sets that underpin a child's ability to learn. Also focuses on supporting a child's literacy skills and incorporates training (with DVD), in Paired Reading, a well-established method for supporting literacy.

www.corambaaf.org.uk/bookshop